D1743807

Contents

Foreword

Jay Nathan has produced a remarkable book. His painstaking and tireless decade of research dedicated to understanding the story of development in Kazakhstan has resulted in a pioneering, comprehensive, and insightful analysis of the political economy of that young republic.

For centuries Britain and Russia played out the so-called Great Game to determine which would control that part of the world reaching from the Caucasus on the west to Burma on the east. They understood the strategic and economic importance of controlling such a key region. Right in the heart of it are the land and the people who today comprise the vast modern nation of Kazakhstan which for almost seventy years was dominated by Soviet control. Out from under Soviet dominance, the countries of Central Asia, including Kazakhstan, are now poised to become influential, independent players themselves in world affairs.

Much of what has been written about the satellite countries which became autonomous after the breakup of the Soviet Union is focused on political issues, like democracy and rule of law. Sadly, there is not enough good literature about economic issues in these countries and that is particularly true concerning Kazakhstan. Thus many students do not learn about Kazakhstan or its economic development challenges and potential. Jay Nathan's exhaustive work provides students and teachers alike, in international relations, economic development, management, and political science, a valuable resource for understanding Kazakhstan, and finally a model for studying other developing nations.

During part of the more than ten years he spent researching and producing this work, Jay lived in Kazakhstan, as a Fulbright scholar, interviewing countless business and government leaders, scouring archives, and databases, and immersing himself in the practical and everyday implications of economic development in Kazakhstan. Based on that research, Jay presents in depth analyses of nine industries essential to Kazakhstan's ongoing economic development. These include the petroleum industry since Kazakhstan's oil reserves are some of the largest in the world. Most importantly, the common theme that integrates Jay's presentation is a focus on how and why Kazakhstan's future progress depends on discarding and outgrowing the outmoded theories and mindsets predominant during Soviet rule. His study illuminates the need for Kazakhstan to embrace globalization and modern management methods in order to achieve ongoing economic development.

Jay Nathan was a member of the School of Management faculty at the University of Scranton for 10 years, between 1983 and 1993. During the 12 years since he left the university he has maintained a close relationship with our institution. When he hosted the president of the University of Kazakhstan on a recent trip to the United States he included in his guest's itinerary a visit to the University of Scranton where he met with numerous teachers, students, and administrators. For that enriching experience we are grateful to Professor Nathan. We are indebted to him even more so for this fine work that will challenge and inform students everywhere for many years to come.

The people of Kazakhstan have an ancient culture and a rich history. Yet for most of the twentieth century they have lived under Soviet domination. With their recently gained freedom from the Soviet Union they have an opportunity for self-determination, both political and economic. If their policy makers and government and business leaders heed Jay Nathan's ideas, analyses, and strategy suggestions, I daresay that Kazakhstan, at the heart of Central Asia, could become a source of regional strength, stability, and prosperity for decades to come. That will be Jay's lasting contribution to scholarship and to management theory in the developing world. I sincerely hope that this impressive book will be widely read.

Rev. Scott Pilarz, S.J., Ph.D.
President
University of Scranton

ACKNOWLEDGEMENTS

I had the good fortune to have received Senior Fulbright Scholarship awards, which enabled me to travel, research, and teach in major universities of the Republic of Kazakhstan; I had the privilege and honor to meet and work with some of the rectors of both public and private universities, supervise master's and doctoral theses, review state and standards for the business education curricula, and most of all, my deepest appreciation and gratitude to my students who were involved in the data collection. Libraries in Almaty, several universities, and government websites, provided valuable data, statistics, and assistance for this research endeavor. My Ph.D. students at the Eurasian National University reviewed parts of the book, and I am thankful for it. Dr. Midori Yamanouchi, Ph.D. professor emeriti of The University of Scranton for editing, and providing critical reviews and thoughtful suggestions on the manuscript, for which I am very grateful.

This book would never be possible without the Senior Fulbright Scholarship awards accorded to the author from the Council for the International Exchange of Scholars in Washington, D.C. During my Fulbright years in Kazakhstan, on several occasions, I had the privilege of meeting His Excellency, Mr. Larry Napper, U.S. Ambassador to Kazakhstan; he encouraged me, on this book project, for which I am thankful. Also, many thanks go to Stephen Guice, Cultural Affairs Officer at the U.S. Embassy. I am also grateful to the St. John's University in Queens, New York City for the research leave and support, which enabled me to teach and research in Kazakhstan for the academic years of 2002-03, 2004 and 2005. I am grateful to Rev. Richard W. Rousseau, S.J., the past Director of The University of Scranton Press, for believing in me and the research on Kazakhstan. I thank Jeff Gainey, the recent past Director of The University of Scranton Press, for his assistance. I am very grateful to Dr. Steven Jones, Associate Provost, The University of Scranton, for his painstaking editing and commitment to see the manuscript in print as a book.

Preface

SINCE THE WORLDWIDE COMMERCIALIZATION of the Internet, the world has experienced, as never before, rapid flow of information from one corner to the other in a variety of ways: text, music, telephony, e-mail, graphics, to name just a few. For the first time in human history, the economic integration of globalization has significant influence on all sovereign nations: small, or large; developed, or emerging, or poor. Both print and visual media are accessible on a daily basis—any time, anywhere—at affordable prices. The world has become a stage, where any event, good news, and bad news flow freely on the Internet, and can be accessed instantaneously by means of a variety of telecommunication devices. What does this mean to peoples and nations who want to improve their lot and create wealth for their nations and societies? There are many benefits, if properly harnessed, especially to poor and developing nations. Because of industrialized nations, who keep their economies dynamic and measure their wealth in terms of goods and services produced each year, by means of Gross National Product (GNP) as an indicator of how well they have done in relation to past years, and in relation to other nations, there has been much attention given to nation building—especially by poor and developing nations—in "management of nations" for harnessing the resources and emerging industries. Since the publication of *Wealth of Nations* by Adam Smith, citizens from all walks of life around the world began to pay attention to the GNPs of all sovereign nations, published each year. That this measurement can be, at times, imperfect or inaccurate is not the issue here; the fact that this can be a score card is sufficient. The premise of this book takes a progressive view of the larger benefits that accrue from industrialization, modernization, and internationalization in a global era.

This book is about Kazakhstan, a large country slightly greater than a third of the size of the United States. Prior to 1991, Kazakhstan for a good part of seventy (70) years was part of the Soviet Union. After the break-up of the Soviet Union, the Republic was the last among the Soviet Central Asia to seek independence from the Russian Federation. I was fortunate to lecture, research, and travel not only in Kazakhstan, but also in other countries of former Soviet Central Asia, approximately for a period of nine months. During that time, I constantly asked myself the following questions: "Why are some countries able to create wealth and increase their GNPs, while others struggle to survive?" "Why are there one hundred countries or so, that do not participate in international trade nor internationalize their domestic businesses?" I was consumed by these issues during my travels abroad.

The answer seems to lie in the "development and growth of industries" and "how proper management can be applied to the industrial development and growth." That is, management at all levels, beginning from the nations' administrators—presidents and prime ministers—down to the state or province, city or village; as well as nations' private and state enterprises. I call these groups "top management", who are the "movers" and "shakers" of nations, and the various industries over which they preside. All nations, including Kazakhstan, are at the crossroads in this day of globalization.

This book is also about how proper management can benefit Kazakhstan and many other developing nations. The present—especially in transitional economies—does compete with past values. Formerly colonized countries suffer from the inherited mindset that prevents them from learning from the developed countries and the free market system. This is a major challenge. The nascent industries, if managed well, can be engines of growth, and therefore can create wealth and promote quality of life for modernization. The details of the emerging industries, their performances thus far, analyses, strategies, evaluation and control of recommended management ideas to modernize, internationalize, and grow in a global era will be presented in the coming chapters.

Chapter 1

How Kazakhstan's Present Competes with Past Values

KAZAKHSTAN LIES in the north of the central Asian republics and is bounded by Russia in the north, China in the east, Kyrgyzstan and Uzbekistan in the south, and the Caspian Sea and part of Turkmenistan in the west. It has almost 1,177 mi (1,894 km) of coastline on the Caspian Sea. Kazakhstan is slightly more than twice the size of Texas. The territory is mostly steppe land with hilly plains and plateaus (Source: National Statistical Agency of Kazakhstan).

Figure 1-1

Source: Michigan State University: Global edge, 2003

Past

Humans have inhabited present-day Kazakhstan since the earliest Stone Age, generally pursuing the nomadic pastoral life for which the region's climate and terrain are best suited. The earliest well-documented

1

state in the region was the Turkic Khanate, which came into existence in the sixth century A.D. The Qarluqs, a confederation of Turkic tribes, established a state in what is now eastern Kazakhstan in 766. In the eighth and ninth centuries, portions of southern Kazakhstan were conquered by Arabs, who also introduced Islam. The Oghuz Turks controlled western Kazakhstan from the ninth through the eleventh centuries; the Kimak and Kipchak peoples, also of Turkic origin, controlled the east at roughly the same time. The large central desert of Kazakhstan is still called Dashti-Kipchak, or the Kipchak Steppe.

In the late ninth century, the Qarluq state was destroyed by invaders who established the large Qarakhanid state, which occupied a region known as Transoxania, the area north and east of the Oxus River (the present-day Syrdarya), extending into what is now China. Beginning in the early eleventh century, the Qarakhanids fought constantly among themselves and with the Seljuk Turks to the south. In the course of these conflicts, parts of present-day Kazakhstan shifted back and forth between the combatants. The Qarakhanids, who accepted Islam and the authority of the Arab Abbasid caliphs of Baghdad during their dominant period, were conquered in the 1130s by the Karakitai, a Turkic confederation from northern China. In the mid-twelfth century, an independent state of Khorazm (also spelled as Khorezm or Khwarazm) along the Oxus River broke away from the weakening Karakitai, but the bulk of the Karakitai state lasted until the invasion of Chinggis (Genghis) Khan in 1219–21.

After the Mongol capture of the Karakitai state, Kazakhstan fell under the control of a succession of rulers of the Mongolian Golden Horde, the western branch of the Mongol Empire. (The horde, or zhuz, is the precursor of the present-day clan, which is still an important element of Kazak society). By the early fifteenth century, the ruling structure had split into several large groups known as khanates, including the Nogai Horde and the Uzbek Khanate.

The Kazaks became a recognizable group in the mid-fifteenth century, when clan leaders broke away from Abul Khayr, leader of the Uzbeks, to seek their own territory in the lands of Semirech'ye, between the Chu and Talas rivers in present-day southeastern Kazakhstan. The first Kazak leader was Khan Kasym (r. 1511–23), who united the Kazak tribes into one people. In the sixteenth century, when the Nogai Horde and Siberian khanates broke up, clans from each jurisdiction joined the Kazaks. The Kazaks subsequently separated into three new hordes: the Great Horde, which controlled Semirech'ye and southern Kazakhstan; the Middle Horde, which occupied north-central Kazakhstan; and the Lesser Horde, which occupied western Kazakhstan.

Russian traders and soldiers began to appear on the northwestern edge of Kazak territory in the seventeenth century, when Cossacks established the forts that later became the cities of Oral (Ural'sk) and Atyrau (Gur'yev). Russians were able to seize Kazak territory because the khanates were pre-occupied by Kalmyk invaders of Mongol origin, who in the late sixteenth century had begun to move into Kazak territory from the east. Forced westward in what they call their Great Retreat, the Kazaks were increasingly caught between the Kalmyks and the Russians. In 1730, Abul Khayr, one of the khans of the Lesser Horde, sought Russian assistance. Although Abul Khayr's intent had been to form a temporary alliance against the stronger Kalmyks, the Russians gained permanent control of the Lesser Horde as a result of his decision. The Russians conquered the Middle Horde by 1798, but the Great Horde managed to remain independent until the 1820s, when the expanding Quqon (Kokand) Khanate to the south forced the Great Horde khans to choose Russian protection, which seemed to them the lesser of two evils.

The Kazaks began to resist Russian control almost as soon as it became complete. The first mass uprising was led by Khan Kene (Kenisary Kasimov) of the Middle Horde, whose followers fought the Russians between 1836 and 1847. Khan Kene is now considered a Kazak national hero (Source: The Library of Congress Country Studies).

Present

Kazakhstan, the largest of the former Soviet republics in territory, excluding Russia itself, possesses enormous fossil fuel reserves as well as plentiful supplies of other minerals and metals. It also is a large agricultural producer of livestock and grain. Kazakhstan's economy rests on the extraction and processing of these natural resources and also on a growing machine-building sector specializing in construction equipment, tractors, agricultural machinery, and some defense equipments, which were all under the control of the Soviet Union in the past. The breakup of the USSR in December 1991 and the collapse in demand for Kazakhstan's traditional heavy industry products resulted in a short-term contraction of the economy, with the steepest annual decline occurring in 1994. In 1995–97, however, the pace of the government program of economic reform and privatization quickened, resulting in a substantial shifting of assets into the private sector. Kazakhstan enjoyed double-digit growth in 2000–01, and a solid 9.5 percent in 2002, thanks largely to its booming energy sector, but also to economic reform, good harvests, and foreign investment. Because of the opening of the Caspian Pipeline Consortium, in 2001, from Western Kazakhstan's Tengiz oilfield, to the Black Sea, it substantially raised export capacity. The country has embarked upon an industrial policy designed to diversify the economy away from over-dependence on the oil sector, by developing light industry. Additionally, the policy aims to reduce the influence of foreign investment and foreign personnel; the government has engaged in several disputes with foreign oil companies over the terms of production agreements, and tensions continue.

Kazakhstan's population is about 14.8 million as of 2002; population per square km. is 5.4; population growth is 1.2%; life expectancy is 66 years; literacy rate is 98.4%; population below minimum subsistence level is 38%; GDP is in U.S. $24.4 billion; GDP growth is 9.5% (based on 2002 data; sources: National Statistical Offices, IMF, World Bank estimates). Kazakhstan is a lower middle-income country with Gross National Income (GNI) per capita of U.S. $1,510. It is the largest country in Central Asia and one of the most sparsely populated in the world.

Kazakhstan has considerable mineral wealth and vast areas of arable land, but many areas of the vast territory cannot be used for agriculture now because of the lack of water. The problem is that, in many areas, when a well is drilled, the water that comes up is salt water, not fresh water. So, as in some parts of China, Kazakhstan needs a serious policy for desalination if she is to use her land effectively.

As mentioned before, this country's economy is highly dependent upon its rich natural resources. In 2002, oil production, transportation, and food processing accounted for about 16 percent of GDP, while exports of oil and gas products accounted for 56 percent of the total. Metallurgy (ferrous and non-ferrous metals) and grains are the only other significant export products. Exports of non-extractive commodities (mainly grain, cotton and meat products) have been stagnant since 2000, and the economy faces the daunting challenge of developing other basic industrial activities, particularly manufacturing most of the things the people need for everyday life, such as garments, kitchen utensils, furniture, and even toys. Currently, they depend on imported goods, handled mostly by Russians. Although income per capita reached U.S. $1510 in 2002, substantial poverty remains. Also, this per capita income figure may be misleading because 70 percent of the population works for the government, showing a real weakness of the private sector in its economy. Preliminary calculations based on the government's minimum level of subsistence reveal an overall poverty rate of 38 percent in 2001. Poverty rates exceed 57 percent in three oblasts (Jambyl, Kyzylorda, and Mangistau). Kazakhstan also has some of the lowest social indicators in the Europe and Central Asia region, including those of access to safe drinking water and the incidence of tuberculosis. In addition, environmental degradation, such as the receding level of the Aral Sea, poses a major challenge for the country.

Since independence in 1991, Kazakhstan has been one of the earliest and most vigorous reformers among the countries of the former Soviet Union. Yet that transition cannot be seen as successful as anticipated. The problem is rooted in the old Soviet mind-set. In the early years of transition, prices were liberalized, trade distortions reduced, and small-and medium-scale enterprises privatized. The government established a basic framework to attract foreign direct investment into its abundant oil and mineral sectors. A serious problem has been observed in the banking sector; namely, following the independence, the banking sector has been experiencing a difficulty in shedding the old government control system, and in adjusting to the global economy.

The recent economic performance is due to a buoyant recovery, which started in 2000, and was led mainly by the oil sector which continued to grow through 2002. Real GDP grew 13.5 percent in 2001 and 9.5 percent in 2002. Agriculture has also shown strong signs of recovery since 1998, especially in the sub-sector of grain. Grain production has increased on average by 46 percent per year during 1998–2002. In spite of significant capital inflows, the currency has been stable and, in real term, has appreciated only slightly against the U.S. dollar, a trend that is expected to continue. Inflation is around seven percent, mainly due to demand pressures over such goods as fruits and vegetables along border countries, as well as due to regional authorities unable to effectively implement regulation.

To ensure that a larger share of the population may benefit from the recent economic growth, the government is looking for ways to improve its spending policies to increase social spending as well as to invest more for general economic growth by diversifying the non-oil sector, particularly the labor-intense sectors, i.e., manufacturing, which is urgently needed for increasing job opportunities and income for the people, as well as to reduce the economy's vulnerability to oil price swings.

From the recent study (2003) undertaken by the World Bank, Kazakhstan's government and consumer expenditures for various sectors are: law and public administration, 28% (551 m); transportation, 7% (135 m); agriculture, 7% (136 m); education, 1% (17.7 m); energy and mining, 17% (322 m); finance, 20% (381 m); health and social services, 3% (53 m); industry and trade, 15% (289 m).

Present Competes with Past Values

Kazakhstan is rather unique among the rest of the former Soviet Union countries such as Poland and others; the dominance of the Soviet Union was much shorter, and also unique among the rest of the developing nations coming out of the colonial era. From the beginning of human history, the earliest form of society is hunting/gathering where people survive from what they can get from what is available naturally. Then, it advanced to the next level, horticultural society, when they gained the knowledge that they can plant seeds to grow food, and therefore surplus was introduced, and that marks the beginning of the exchange of food and other things, by the barter system at first, which led to the introduction of specialization. And, this introduction of surplus was what led to social stratification. When a horticultural society acquired the knowledge that they can replenish the soil, it advanced to the next level, agricultural society, which may be the early and the later stages. Then, as we all know, that is followed by the next level, the industrial society, and then, the post-industrial society. In any society that followed this common natural process, manufacturing activities accompanied specialization, from limited to a larger and more complex, systematic types of manufacturing to fill its own domestic needs and for foreign trade.

Observing Kazakhstan's economy, it seems as if it is not natural that manufacturing activities are so lacking. This may be explained by the fact that, due to a variety of environmental factors, different parts of Kazakhstan remained in a traditional nomadic lifestyle, at the quasi-foragers level, and not sedentary, even at the time when the vast area fell under Soviet rule about a hundred years ago. Since the members of those nomadic tribes could buy things elsewhere and bring them back for their own use or sale for profit, thus, they acquired the necessary skills to be successful traders. The rest of the population, who are sedentary, could buy from them what they needed; hence they did not particularly become involved in manufacturing things they needed themselves. So, this would explain why, in general, manufacturing activities lagged behind in Kazakhstan, and that left the society with a uniquely mixed level of development, unlike most other societies. In addition, the lack of agricultural business, in spite of the large size of the land, as discussed elsewhere, is due to the quality of water available for agriculture. This fact also contributed to the lack of manufacturing activities, i.e., processing food, etc.

Of course, the Soviet administration was the primary reason that Kazakhstan did not develop a manufacturing sector that could produce the variety of things they needed for everyday life. As in any other society under Soviet control, it interrupted the natural development of Kazakhstan's culture, i.e., the way of life, particularly her social institutions. In addition, the Soviets used Kazakhstan as just a part of the union to benefit only the Soviet regime by extracting abundant raw material, such as oil, natural gas and other mineral resources from Kazakhstan for the benefit of the Soviet and also used Kazakhstan as its market to sell the finished products, in a fashion similar to what colonial powers did to their colonies but in a more extreme way because of the geographic proximity. As a consequence, the natural diffusion and adaptation process were interrupted by the Soviet control. When a new knowledge is introduced to any society, either from within or from outside the society, it goes through an adaptation process to benefit the society. But how successful, or how beneficial the end result is to the society depends on the society's culture, particularly its value system, the level of knowledge, as well as its existing social institutions. So, in the end, some societies failed to yield any benefit from the diffusion process by faulty adaptation, and in many cases, even caused disharmony and other disruption to the society by misusing whatever knowledge was introduced to the society. Some societies have indeed used any new knowledge to advance the society and improve its people's quality of life very well. An interesting example is that of China: when they first invented what the West calls gun powder, knowing that they could use it to make guns, they refused to do so, and wanted to maintain that knowledge for beautiful fireworks. That is, it is the society's cultural value that affects the adaptation itself.

Returning to the problem of the lack of manufacturing industry in Kazakhstan, it is evident that it was caused by the major factors discussed earlier. The most important factor was, obviously, the Soviet Union's taking over and preventing Kazakhstan's natural progress and forcing her Marxist system upon Kazakhstan. Additionally, the Soviet Union used Kazakhstan as a piece of her union so that the Soviets could take the greatest advantage as a result. Why should the Soviet Union help Kazakhstan to develop manufacturing activities? The Soviets wanted to keep Kazakhstan dependent on the Soviet Union as the supplier of natural resources, e.g., oil, natural gas, minerals, etc., as well as keeping Kazakhstan as a market to sell what the Soviet Union manufactured as finished products. Since the Soviet Union had enough power to impose on Kazakhstan, even the type of manufacturing that was allowed to continue was not necessarily for the benefit of the people of Kazakhstan. So, the society's need after her independence with regard to manufacturing activities that would have naturally developed whether they be garment, utensil, furniture, etc., did not exist because the Soviet Union did not allow that to happen.

For a matter of comparison, in a country like Poland, where the Soviet dominance came and lasted less than half a century, although they were kept down during that period, for the Polish people to pick up where they were forced to drop off was possible quite quickly, because they were already in the industrial period when the Soviet dominance started. In other words, the difficulty of Kazakhstan is due to these two factors: her unique historical background, and the century-long Soviet control.

In addition, for Kazakhstan, another problem preventing her timely rapid acculturation with the rest of the free world is that, in spite of the high literacy rate of the people, apparently the former Soviet-type education did not educate the people to acquire more general knowledge about the rest of the world. The people have no idea what the real free market means, what open competition means, the principle of supply and demand, let alone what the capitalist system, market system is, or what democracy means. For that reason, a great many ordinary people came to believe what the end of Marxism meant. How such misconceptions could be corrected would be a daunting challenge for the new leaders. It is truly regrettable that so many people seem to believe that the privatization is akin to that of seizure of wealth and corruption. People jokingly refer to *privatizatsiya* as *prikhvatizatsiya*, or "grabbing" of assets by former state ministerial higher-ups, using their proximity and control in the bureaucratic chain to convert state factories, otdelenie, and coffers into profit-oriented self-interests. Such cynical views from the peoples of the former Soviet Central Asian countries reflect a general discontent, and in some cases alienation, toward the value of individual ownership. This type of widely shared misconception is a very serious problem for Kazakhstan to develop herself as a member of the global economy.

Moreover, under the Soviet system, everyone was equal, quite contrary to the meritocratic system which values the competency of individuals. Any contemporary society needs that type of thinking, which encourages individual members of the society to develop his/her potentials fully, and the society can use their competence in numerous fields where it is needed in the world today. Meritocracy provides incentives for individuals to do so as well, because it values and rewards each person's competency, which can contribute to the society's well-being. Under the egalitarian society, if everyone is equal (not for the opportunity but the competence), to be clever, rather than excellent, is encouraged, and, in order to move up, one must be a good sycophant and a good opportunist. So, as we have seen, in the societies under the Soviet system, there was no sense of integrity as well. It was the reason many intelligent people outside the Marxist system, who had a chance to observe it, could foresee the fall of the Soviet Union more than a quarter century earlier.

At any rate, to shed such a dysfunctional mentality is not going to be easy for the people of Kazakhstan. However, perhaps their exposure to and learning more about what is going on in the rest of the world will help, but that may take time. And, for that, more open-minded, broadly educated leaders will be absolutely necessary. In short, it is imperative that the people of Kazakhstan, particularly the more educated among them, shed the Soviet mentality in every sense of the term, if Kazakhstan hopes to prosper in the future, if not forever, by adapting successfully to her constantly changing environment, whether it may be a natural, human, or intellectual environment.

Chapter 2

Kazakhstan's Oil Supply Chain Management Challenges

KAZAKHSTAN IS ENDOWED with rich oil reserves, which provide an important source of revenues for stable economic growth and improvement of the country's living standard. This chapter addresses the challenge the Republic of Kazakhstan faces in managing its oil supply chain. The country's capacity for refining crude oil is minimal, and a substantial portion of that refining capacity is outside the Republic; added to that, most of the pipelines and refineries to export oil to international markets are jointly managed by the Republic and multinational corporations (MNCs). Thus there are political, technological, and financial risks for the republic's oil supply chain.

Introduction

Kazakhstan has considerable deposits of oil; however, the country faces a serious disadvantage of not having any direct access to the open sea, as the Caspian Sea is landlocked. While her oil industry's *upstream cost*, i.e., the cost for exploration, development, and production of crude oil, may be similar to that of most other oil producing nations, its *downstream cost*, i.e., transportation of crude oil to the refinery, refining, and transportation to markets in particular, is more costly (Sridharan, Canines, and Patterson; 2005). For Kazakhstan to transport the oil to world markets, the industry has to depend on pipelines (Cavanaugh, 1999) through other countries.

11

Also, maintaining such an operation requires a large number of skilled workers, but Kazakhstan does not have enough of them.

As in other oil producing nations, Kazakhstan's oil industry revenues directly depend on the worldwide prices for oil and oil products, based on supply and demand; and revenues depend on the cost of production and transporting the final product to customers (Rasizade, 1999). For Kazakhstan's oil supply chain, the physical distribution infrastructure connecting supplies of crude oil to refineries and to the world markets through pipelines, has been challenging and costly. Moreover, currently Kazakhstan is equipped with only a few refineries, and therefore the major portion of Kazakhstan's crude oil is being refined in Russia. Recently, China has invested heavily in the construction of pipelines across the Republic of Kazakhstan to supply the increased demand for oil in China. Thus Kazakhstan has to manage political, technical, and financial risks in the integration of her oil supply chain (Gaudenzi and Borghesi, 2006; Lockamy and McCormack, 2004).

In the era of rapid technological development and globalization, it is imperative that every nation adapts to such an environment. *Supply chain management* has become an important means for sustaining a competitive advantage for all successful industries and businesses (Magretta, 1998). The objective of every supply chain, including the global oil industry, is to maximize the overall value generated. The *value* a supply chain generates [to an organization, or to a nation] is the difference between what the final product is worth to the customer, and the effort the supply chain expends in filling the customer's request. For most commercial supply chains, *value* will be strongly correlated with *supply chain profitability*, the difference between the revenue generated from the customer and the overall cost across the supply chain (Chopra and Meindl, 2003; Lee, 2002; Cavinato, 2002). The Republic of Kazakhstan will do well to monitor—especially to sustain growth—the overall *value* of her oil supply chain in the coming years.

Oil Producing Countries and Global Supply Chains

Energy makes the wheels of global supply chains go round (Bud La Londe, 2006). A typical oil supply chain begins with the crude oil producer; next, the oil moves to the refiner, the transporter, the retailer, and finally to the gas pump where a customer receives the product. The top world oil producers are Saudi Arabia, Russia, the United States, Iran, Mexico, China, Canada, United Arab Emirates, Venezuela, Norway, Kuwait, Nigeria, Brazil, Kazakhstan, and Iraq. The Organization of the Petroleum Exporting Countries (OPEC) controls major crude oil supplies to the world. OPEC influences the price of crude oil by setting production quotas. The values (revenue opportunities) are added by processing and chemically changing the crude oil, which is called "refining." A 42-gallon barrel of crude oil makes about 19½ gallons of gasoline, 9 gallons of fuel oil, 4 gallons of jet fuel, and 11 gallons of other products, including lubricants, kerosene, asphalt, and petrochemical feed-stocks to make plastics. This adds up to more than 42 gallons because of refinery gain (www.gravmag.com, 2006). It is important to note that greater economic rewards can be gained *only* with well-integrated global oil supply chain management.

Oil Production Sharing Agreement and Risks in Kazakhstan

The Ministry of Energy and Mineral Resources of Kazakhstan, and the Ministry of Fuel and Energy of Russia periodically set quotas for Kazakhstan's oil flow through Russian territory. For example, on December 25, 2000, the quota for Kazakhstan was set at 17.3 million tons. The memorandum between Kazakhstan and Russia of October 9, 2000, sets the principle of "a single route," whose sole operator is the Kazakh Oil Company. Annual quotas depend mainly on the political relations between the two nations.

Besides politics, there is also a technical risk factor, i.e., the high degree of pipeline wear and deterioration, which may hamper the effectiveness and quality of services provided to exporting countries. In addition, the lack of proper maintenance of these oil pipelines exists primarily due to the fact that the large number of well-trained local technicians and engineers required is not available today (*Doing Business with Kazakhstan*, 2004).

Kazakhstan's oil pipeline systems were built in the '70s (more than 60% of oil pipelines of the Western branch, to be exact), and the rest in the '80s (75% of the Eastern branch). Thus at the end of the year 2000, 55% of the pipelines were 10 to 20 years old, and 12% had been used for more than 30 years. Only 1% has been used for less than 10 years. As time goes by, those pipelines are getting even older, and that means not only the risk and cost of maintaining them would be larger, but also the situation presents serious technical problems as well for the Republic of Kazakhstan (Petroleumjournal.com, 2006).

Kazakhstan's Oil Fields and Production

Mangistau and Atyrau oblasts (provinces) are the main oil producing areas in Kazakhstan (see Figure 2-1). They account for more than 70% of the total oil extracted in the Republic. The other three extracting regions, Aktyubinsk, Kyzlorda, and Zapadno-Kazakhstanskaya, account for the remainder. International oil projects have taken the form of joint ventures, production sharing agreements, and exploration/field agreements.

Figure 2-1
Production by Regions

(in thousand tons)	1998	1999	2000	2001
Crude oil, thousand tons	**23,818.7**	**26,735.8**	**30,647.9**	**36,060.0**
Aktyubinsk	2,640.8	2,326.7	2,701.1	3,405.3
Atyrauskaya	11,135.1	12,359.3	13,422.0	15,589.5
Zapadno-Kazakhstanskaya	-	-	13.5	49.4
Kyzylordinskaya	3,007.8	3,928.1	533.8	6,172.8
Mangistauskaya	7,035.0	8,121.7	9,173	10,843.0

Source: National Statistics Agency of Kazakhstan, 2005

Oil is recovered from 55 fields. The largest of these fields are: Tengiz (some 1 billion tons of predicted oil reserves); Karachaganak (340 million tons in oil reserves, more than 1.2 billion tons in gas condensates, and more than 1.3 trillion cubic meters of natural gas); Uzen (with over 1.5 billion tons of geological hydrocarbon reserves, of which more than 200 million tons are extractable); and Kumkola (with 350 million tons of oil reserves, of which 80 million tons of oil and 75 billion cubic meters of natural gas are proven). The Caspian and Aral Sea shelf also contain significant reserves. Currently, there are only three major refineries in Kazakhstan: Atyrau, Shymkent, and Pavlodar (see Figure 2-2). The major oil producing and refining areas are shown in Figure 2-1 and Figure 2-3.

Figure 2-2
Design and Delivery Capacities of Major Refineries

Plant	Design Capacity *mln tons*	Actual Deliveries *mln tons*	Per Month		Per Day	
			Design, *thousand tons*	Actual, *thousand tons*	Design, *thousand tons*	Actual, *thousand tons*
Shymkent Oil Refinery	6.5	3.6	590	326.8	19.7	10.9
Pavlodar Oil Refinery	7.5	2.3	677	189.5	22.6	6.3
Atyrau Oil Refinery	4.6	2.7	418	245.4	14	8.2

Source: National Statistics Agency of Kazakhstan, 2005

- Pavlodar (a foreign investor was given a management concession in 1997; the plant has been under government control since summer 1999) processes mainly light crude from Siberia, and supplies the northern region of Kazakhstan;
- Atyrau belongs to Kazakhoil, processing heavy domestic oil, and supplies the western region;
- Shymkent was mostly sold (95 percent) to private investors in 1996. It processes dedicated crude from the region (Kumkol, Aktyubinsk, Turkmen fields) and supplies the south, particularly Almaty.

Major Oil Pipelines and Their Routes Map

Here are the various Kazak pipelines and their routes:

Figure 2-3
Map of Major Pipelines

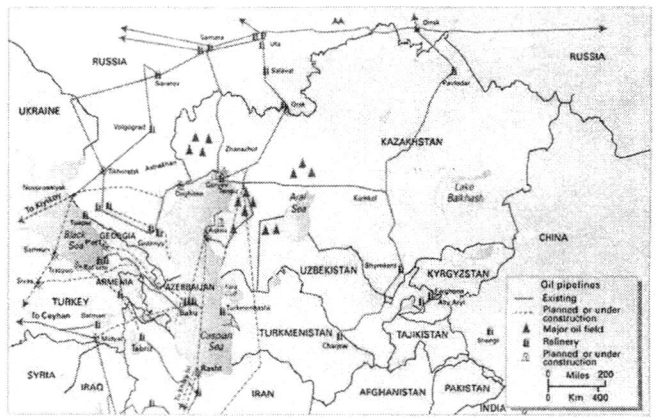

Oil Pipelines Infrastructure in Central Asia
Source: Adapted from KazakhstanOil and Gas
International Conference Proceedings, 2002

The major pipelines are identified by the Kazakhstan Ministry of Power, Industry, and Trade as the projected priority export routes for oil in the following order.

1. Atyrau-Samara pipeline: The possibilities for oil exports along the Atyrau-Samara oil pipeline are restricted by its throughput capacity and by the quota set by Russia. This is a constraining factor for the growth of both crude oil production and export supplies. To increase the throughput capacity from 10 to 15 million tons per year, a series of technical measures in Kazakhstan and Russia are being taken at a cost of 22 million dollars;

2. Tengiz-Novorossisk oil pipeline: The Caspian Pipeline Consortium's (CPC) oil export pipeline project is a short-term priority westward. This project ensures an independent outlet for Kazakhstan's oil exports to the Black Sea and opens up opportunities for the attraction of foreign investments in the oil-and-gas sector. The necessary agreements for the project participants have already been signed and operations initiated;

3. Trans-Caspian pipeline: Planned to follow a route through the Black Sea to Turkey, the Trans-Caspian oil pipeline project is considered to be a priority. The oil pipeline will stretch from Western Kazakhstan to an outlet on the Mediterranean (the Turkish port of Ceyhan) via the Caspian Sea. The territory of Azerbaijan, Georgia and Turkey creates risks for the project due to the complicated mountainous terrain and water barriers, and the need to cross conflict-prone zones;

4. Kazakhstan-China pipeline: Since 2004, in the Kazakhstan section of the Caspian Sea, the volume of the crude oil production has increased. The export oil pipeline of the CPC alone cannot meet the demand for oil transportation infrastructure. Preliminary engineering and economic calculations have shown that an oil pipeline eastward to China is a promising and economically favorable project. The Kazakhstan-China oil pipeline project can, simultaneously, meet Kazakhstan's national security interests, and provide an outlet to meet China's growing demand for oil. The oil pipeline's route will pass over the territory of Kazakhstan, and China will guarantee the project funding. The downside of the project is that the People's Republic of China can potentially control the price paid for the oil;

5. Persian Gulf-Iranian oil pipeline: The Persian Gulf-Iranian oil pipeline provides another possible oil pipeline route to the south. However, severe competition from OPEC countries can bring about a reduction in the price paid for oil from the Persian Gulf. Consequently, a reduced load on the oil pipeline may occur at some time in the future due to low profitability in that market. No terms for investment mobilization for this project have yet been defined;

6. Arabian Sea-Trans-Asian oil pipeline: The Trans-Asian oil pipeline via Kazakhstan-Turkmenistan-Afghanistan-Pakistan to an outlet in the Arabian Sea is politically highly risky, since it passes over the territory of Afghanistan. Currently, consideration is being given to the basic question of how the funding will be organized for the project.

Kazakhstan's Oil Production and Distribution Costs

A multitude of different schemes exist for dividing oil revenues between the host country and the foreign partner. The usual target for distribution of revenue from production to market is about 85% to the host country and 15% to the oil company. This ratio can be construed in a variety of different ways with different types of contractual forms; it also depends on the host country's laws and preferences, but in general oil companies target this ratio. This number has varied over the years. For example, in Saudi Arabia the ratio is much higher in favor of the Saudis due to huge reserves and lower production costs. In the Caspian, the ratio is likely to be lower due to additional transport costs of getting the oil out of the region, i.e., pipeline construction costs and transit fees, and political risks in the area. Part of the problem with signing contracts with Caspian nations has been the nation's unwillingness to recognize the economic necessity of decreasing the ratio (Feiveson, 1998).

The upstream breakdown of costs is about 10% for exploration to find an economical field (odds are about 1 in 10 holes drilled will hit a commercial-sized field), 80% (or higher) to develop the find, and 10% in operating costs to produce the oil. Exploration costs are cash expenditures, which include payments for exploration licenses to the host countries. Development costs are capital costs depreciated over time, and operating costs pay for themselves with the sales of crude oil production. Downstream costs include transportation of crude to the refinery, refining, transportation of products to market, and marketing.

If one were to examine the cost breakdown of a gallon of gas (called petrol in some countries) averaged around the world, from ground to market, the distribution would be approximately:

- 2.5% for exploration,
- 12.5% (or more) for production and development,
- 20% to the host government,
- 2.5% for transportation to a refinery,
- 7.5% for refining,

- 2.5% to transport to market,
- 2.5% for marketing, and
- 50% in taxes to the consumer at the pump.

For example, the costs per barrel for export of Tengiz oil are: lifting costs (the costs to get crude oil extracted from below the surface and bringing it to ground level) $2.00, pipeline costs $1.42, transit fee $3.00, shipping by oil tanker (including other means) $1.23. The total comes to $7.65.

Figure 2-4
Comparison of Transport Costs per Barrel of Kazakh Oil

Route	Cost to Port	Black Sea Tanker	Second Pipeline	Final Tanker	Total Cost
Tengiz Novorossiysk	$1.42			$1.23	$2.65
Samsun Ceyhan	$1.42	$0.40	$0.88	$0.76	$3.46
Novorossiysk-Bosporus Bypass	$1.42	$0.40	$0.59	$0.76	$3.17
Turkmenistan – Kharg	$1.57			$0.93	$2.50

Source: KazakhOil Report, 2005

Kazakhstan's Oil Supply Chain Management Challenges

In Kazakhstan the preferred contract form is a joint venture between a foreign firm and a state enterprise, generally KazakhOil, which is the state oil company. In a joint venture both the state enterprise and the foreign firm invest stated amounts of capital, which can take various forms, including physical assets and rights to land. Risk is shared in proportion to capital invested. The amount of control the foreign firm has is usually limited, and in some cases joint ventures are little more than contracts for procurement.

Kazakhstan has two separate pipeline networks: a crude oil pipeline from Western Siberia supplies Pavlodar and Shymkent, while Atyrau runs solely domestic crude from northwest Kazakhstan. The current pipeline system is fragmented and does not link the east and the west of the country, nor does it move petroleum from oil producing fields in the west of the country to the Pavlodar or Shymkent refineries located in the north and the east. The domestic pipeline's capacity will not cope with the anticipated significant volume increases the Republic hopes to be producing in the years to come. At present some of Kazakhstan's production is exported by means of barges to Baku, Azerbaijan, where it is fed into the Azerbaijan pipeline network system and sent to world markets (Rasizade, 1999). The existing pipeline networks will require large investments, if Kazakhstan is to develop its crude oil and gas potential to the fullest.

Kazakhstan's major oil ports are: Atyrau and Aktau; major oil export pipelines are: Tengiz-Novorossiisk (Russia); Uzen-Atyrau-Samara (Russia); the Kenkyak-Orsk (Russia) line that transports oil from the Aktyubinsk fields to the Orsk refinery; and the Caspian Pipeline Consortium (CPC) that transports oil from Western Kazakhstan to the Black Sea at Novorossiysk (Baker and McKenzie, 2002).

Even though the Republic has upgraded its overall educational system, especially the post-secondary curricula, degree offerings, and the academic rigor modeled after the Western-type system, there is still a paucity of engineers and technicians to maintain and to sustain the growth of the oil industry. The benefits of an increased number of educated personnel would be enormous for the proper management of the entire supply chain activities; it is a strategic necessity for the Republic of Kazakhstan to leverage and sustain future oil revenues.

Current Issues in the Global Energy Market

In recent years, demand for energy has surged. This unrelenting increase has helped fuel global economic growth, but placed considerable pressure on suppliers augmented by geopolitics, and other disruptive factors. On the demand side, increased energy security and environmental concerns may lead to changes in consuming countries' energy policies. These uncertainties have been reflected in the market through volatility and high prices (Birol, 2006). Daniel Yergin of Cambridge Energy Research

Associates Inc. (CERA) during a symposium on "The Economics and Geopolitics of Russian Energy" at Georgetown University in Washington, D.C. on October 29, 2007, forecasted that oil prices are becoming increasingly decoupled from the fundamentals of supply and demand (Yergin, 2007).

Policy Implications for the Leadership in Kazakhstan

Kazakhstan is not a major player in geopolitics. OPEC member states and Russia have political clout in the global energy market. Russia, Kazakhstan's northern neighbor, not only has huge oil reserves on her own, but also controls the refining capacities, as well as some of the flows of refined oil from Kazakhstan to world markets. However, for the young republic, the rich deposit of oil is a blessing; at the same time, it can easily be squandered by mismanagement and bad public policy. Fortunately, in today's global world—armed with first-class business know-how and with lessons learned from other oil producing nations—it is possible for the leadership of Kazakhstan to take a long-term view of proven crude oil deposits in the Caspian Sea and within the sovereign republic of Kazakhstan.

Chapter 3

The Gas Industry: Infra-structural Challenges

Introduction

Kazakhstan is ranked 33d on the list of the 71 gas producing countries. However, up to 40% of produced gas is lost in the fields due to poorly developed gas pipeline and storage systems. Kazakhstan has no funds to create the required production facilities it needs for gas processing, storage and transfer, while production of oil, the major export commodity in the country, continues to grow. This results in the flaring of associated gas. Investors are not interested in a commodity for which there are no receptacles, and additional investment in gas processing seems unprofitable to date. The major part of FDI invested in the oil and gas sector has been done in the frameworks of three major projects: the Caspian Sea Offshore Development Project with a total investment of 600 million US$, the Karachaganak gas field development project with a total investment of $4 billion, and the Tengiz Field Exploration with a total investment of $20 billion over the 40-year contract period. Karachaganak is currently the biggest international investment in Kazakhstan. It is a project that is important for the future of Kazakhstan and her success to date stems from the partnership that has been forged between international companies, the government, and the people of Kazakhstan (See Figure 3-3).

The gas industry has a growth strategy. It aims to enter the top ten leading producers of oil and gas by 2015. But to attain this objective the country's gas industry has to resolve its problems of infrastructure development, and export routes. The mission of the gas industry is to provide effective and transparent development of oil and gas to achieve stable economic growth and improve Kazakhstan's national wealth.

Figure 3-1
Rates of Gas Consumption Growth in Europe

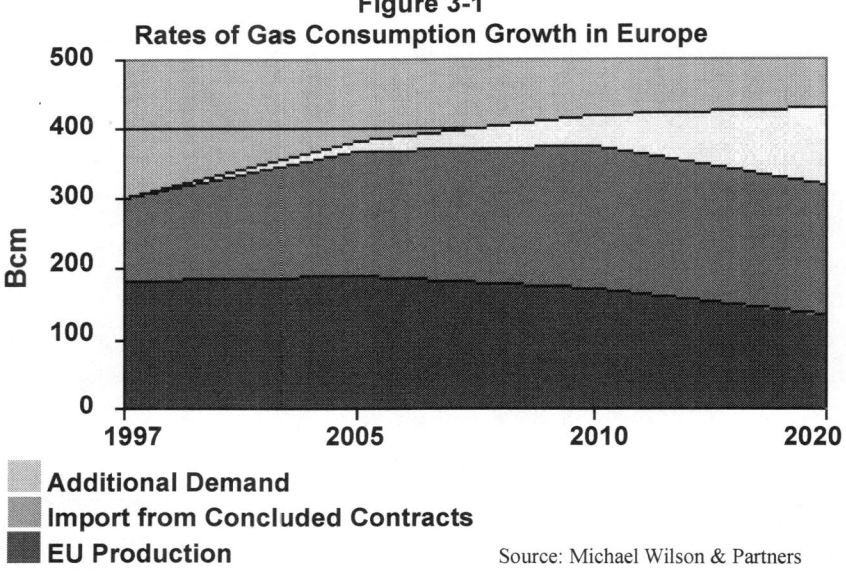

Additional Demand
Import from Concluded Contracts
EU Production   Source: Michael Wilson & Partners

Kazakhstan is also engaged in modernizing her economy and infrastructure, and a free market in energy resources that will encourage foreign investment to explore oil and gas resources. The gas industry's development, growth, and maturity have a long life-cycle, and along with it require capital intensity and developed infrastructure. All this is aggravated by a mix of mismanagement and bureaucracy at all levels of administration. Major foreign players such as Chevron, ExxonMobil, Texaco, Agip and a few others (British Gas, LUKOIL, CNPC, etc.) play highly significant roles in the country's oil and gas industries, so that their status will remain unchanged into the future. The four foreign companies, British Gas, Eni, ChevronTexaco and LUKOIL, have a number of other long-term investment projects in Kazakhstan. They are committed to the economic development of the country and have been contributing tremendously to the community in the regions where they operate and to the country as a whole.

Trends in the Gas Industry

Royal Dutch/Shell in its project "Long-term energy scenarios," presented in 2001, forecasted a shift from oil to gas in the next 10 years. Shell projected that by 2030 the share of oil as an energy source will fall drastically down to 25%, as it will be overtaken by gas and other alternative energy sources. The same projection has been done by British Petroleum, BP, which also is committed to the development of alternative energy sources, and suggests a new interpretation of the BP abbreviation as Beyond Petroleum.

The world's gas consumption has been growing steadily. For ten years it has grown by 18.9 percent from 1931.2 billion cubic meters in 1989 to 2292.6 billion in 1999. Another 30 to 40% increase is expected by 2030. The gas share in the world energy balance increased in just one year, from 23.66 percent in 1998 to 24.1 percent in 1999 and to 32.5 percent in 2005. At the same time, gas production in the major countries of Europe, Asia and America went down.

The increasing gas share in overall primary energy consumption can be explained by two reasons. The first one is ecology. Gas combusting products contain fewer admixtures than the other fuels. The same level of energy derived from burning gas saves 50 percent of carbon emission relative to coal and 30 percent relative to oil. The other reason is deregulation of the gas market in the United States and the United Kingdom.

The market reforms have led to price reduction and therefore growth of demand. For example, the share of gas in the total energy consumption was 22.7 percent in 1980 in the United Kingdom. Since then the government implemented reforms and large-scale privatization in the country. In 1990 the gas share increased to 23.9 percent and in 1998 it reached 37.5 percent.

There is another reason that causes gas use by generator companies. Advances in technology led to the construction of new, more efficient generators, which use gas as a fuel. North America and Europe together consume more than half of the total world gas consumption. The tendency towards increasing gas demand and consumption is preserved throughout Europe (See Figure 3-1). It is seen from figure 3-1, the demand is projected to exceed production of gas, which means that the European Union will be in search of new sources for gas imports. Analysts also project an increasing shortfall between the demand and supply of liquefied natural gas (LNG) in Japan, the Republic of Korea, and Taiwan, which in 2010 is estimated to reach 44 million tons or about 60 Bcm, and could reach 100 Bcm by 2020 because of declining popular support for nuclear power generation.

For China, the demand for natural gas that is not met by domestic production is estimated to be 60 Bcm by 2010, and is expected to rapidly reach 160 Bcm by 2020. Depending on various factors, particularly China's energy policy and the scale of efforts to move away from coal towards cleaner sources of energy, the demand for natural gas could be even higher—only the three northeastern provinces of China are projected to consume between 20 Bcm and 40 Bcm of natural gas by 2020. These estimates and projections allow one to foresee the regional demand for imported natural gas to be about 260-300 Billion Cubic Meters (Bcm). That is why "enormously rich Central Asia and Kazakhstan" are seen as future critical players in the world's gas industry. Figure 3-2 shows gas reserves distribution in the world.

In a statement issued in July 2001, the OPEC Secretary in Vienna stated that Kazakhstan would soon join the ranks of the top oil and gas producers, even catching up to world leader Saudi Arabia. The same idea

Figure 3-2
Gas Reserves Distribution in the World

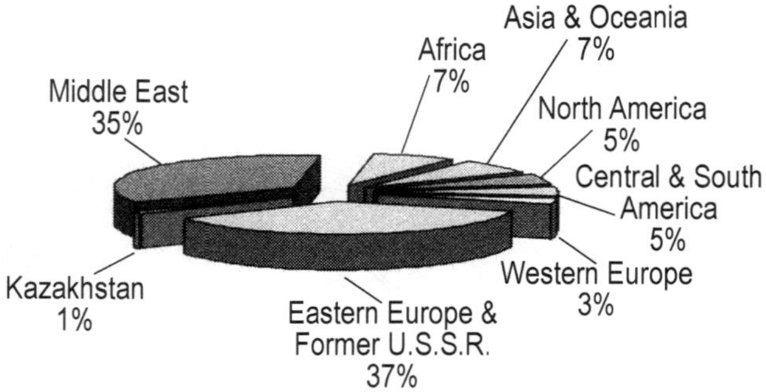

Source: Michael Wilson & Partners

was expressed by Daniel Yergin, Chairman of the Cambridge Energy Research Associates in the USA in 2001, who said, "As new producers in Central Asia are rejoining the economy and tensions rise in the Middle East, the supply of oil and natural gas is becoming more important, along with new investments to ensure that supply."

Figure 3-3: Gas Reserve Deposits in Kazakhstan

NAME OF THE DEPOSIT	RESERVES bln cubic meters
TENGIZ	707.5
KARACHAGANAK	
Solute Gas	239.3
Free Gas	1329.6
URICHTAU	
Solute Gas	0.5
Free Gas	39.8
ZHANAZHOL	
Solute Gas	25.6
Free Gas	25.6

Source: "Gas Industry of Kazakhstan," *Caspian Journal*, October 2000

The Oil and Gas industry plays a vital role in Kazakhstan, as it brings around 40% of hard currency revenues for the country. The structure of Kazakhstan's exports is shown in Figure 9. Over half of the hard currency revenues that Kazakhstan could potentially receive are flared together with the associated gas by oil producing companies. The reason is the following.

Despite Kazakhstan being rich in both, oil and natural gas, historically the gas industry was underdeveloped. More than a century ago (1896), when oil production commenced in Kazakhstan, associated gas was not taken into account. During the Soviet times, gas storage and processing infrastructure was developed, but the power brokers in Moscow were interested in abundant and cheap Turkmen and Uzbek gas, for which transit gas pipelines were laid in the western (a twist of fate) regions of Kazakhstan. This explains why Kazakhstan, possessing huge oil and gas reserves, has only low-capacity gas processing plants which are unable to meet her internal needs: the country imports more than half of the gas consumed by the economy from neighboring countries on stiff terms. The estimates of the gas reserves are: prospected natural gas of 1.7 bln cu m, forecasted reserves including those of the Caspian shelf are estimated at 13 bln tons of oil and gas condensate and 6 bln cu m of natural gas.

Figure 3-4: Karachaganak Integrated Organization's Output in 2001

Gas Production	3.75 Billion Cubic Meters
Condensate Production	4 Million Tons
Social Investments	$20 Million

Source: Karachaganak Integrated Organization

More than 40% of Kazakhstan's gas reserves are located in one field, the giant Karachaganak field in Northwest Kazakhstan, which is an extension of Russia's Orenburg field. Karachaganak (see Figure 3-4) is one of the world's largest oil and gas condensate fields. It covers an area of 280 sq km and holds more than 1.2 trillion tons of oil and condensate and more than 21.35 trillion cubic meters of gas. The expansion of the field is overseen by four international partners—British Gas Group and Eni of Italy each with a 32.5% interest, ChevronTexaco of the USA with 20% and LUKOIL of Russia with 15%. Together they form the Karachaganak Integrated Organization (KIO). In Kazakhstan KIO operates as Karachaganak Petroleum Operating JV (KPO).

Currently, Kazakhstan is pinning her hopes on the development of the Amangeldy and other gas fields in southern Kazakhstan. The Amangeldy and nearby Ayrykty fields in the Jambyl region of southern Kazakhstan have estimated natural gas reserves of more than 777 Bcf, which would be enough to provide uninterrupted natural gas supplies to the southern regions of the country for at least 12 years. Kazakhstan started work at the Amangeldy deposit in the spring of 2001, and began drilling the first of four wells in August 2001. Complete development of the field will cost approximately $770 million, with production started in 2003. Kazakhstan's officials hope to become independent of Uzbek natural gas supplies by 2010.

The major weakness of the strategy in the gas sector is the governmentally regulated production and distribution of the natural gas, which hamper the development of a free market economy, targeted by Kazakhstan and deter foreign investment inflow. The fact is that gas transmission is regulated by the government and is forced to preserve the tariffs as low as possible and the companies cannot invest in the development of gas transmission. These companies are unable to pay for gas supplies because they are forced to charge low prices and do not collect even these prices from many customers.

Figure 3-5
Gas Production in 2001 as Compared with Other Metals

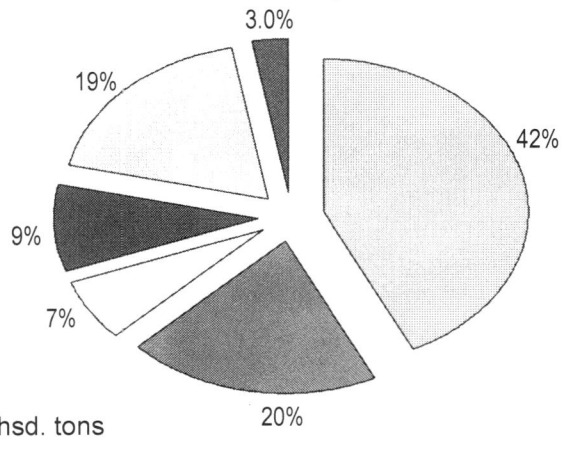

Coal, thsd. tons	42%
Petroleum, inclucing gas condensate, thsd. tons	20%
Natural Gas, min. cubic M	7%
Iron (Commercial) ore, thsd. tons	9%
Steel, thsd. tons	19%
Zinc-Lead Ore, thsd. tons	3%

Source: Kazakhstan State Committee for Statistics and Analysis

Thus the major issue facing Kazakhstan is how to privatize the distribution of gas. This is politically difficult because of public opposition to higher retail prices. Private investors will not purchase these companies, however, until a regulatory regime is in place that will allow them with some certainty to charge and collect reasonable prices.

Kazakhstan must also decide on how to structure her gas sector, which involves complex economic and geo-political issues. For example, should the government attempt to reduce its dependency on gas imports by building new pipelines between its production and consuming areas? If imports continue, who should negotiate with the foreign suppliers—the government, the individual distribution companies, or the transmission company?

Kazakhstan inherited pieces of the old systems that were not integrated. She has to develop new structures, enterprises, and organizations to operate and manage these systems. These systems suffered due to low tariffs, a high degree of non-payment or barter payment, and thus a lack of funds for payments to suppliers.

Statistics, Structure, and Scope in Kazakhstan's Gas Industry

The main peculiarity of Kazakhstan's gas reserve structure is that the majority of deposits under development are ranked as small. The total reserves of each of them do not exceed 1.5% of the total gas reserves. Some 14 of 18 small deposits have initial reserves of less than 1 billion cu meters of gas, and their total reserves are only 4.2 billion cu meters. Figure 3-3 represents the distribution of Kazakhstan's gas reserves among the largest gas deposits. At the same time, the reserves with unique oil and gas condensate deposits, Karachaganak, amount to more than 1,330 bln cu meters of gas. This represents 84% of the current reserves of all the deposits under development, and almost 40% of all gas reserves in Kazakhstan.

Despite the fact that the country is abundant in reserves of natural gas, it is forced to import more than half of its consumption. This is because of the location of its transmission pipelines that were built to serve the needs of the Soviet Union rather than Kazakhstan. The reserves of gas are found in the country's large oil fields as "associated" gas in the northwestern part of the country near the Caspian Sea. Future production from these fields could be as large as 30 billion cubic meters (BCM) per year.

In order to remove disincentives to the development of the country's natural gas industry, in August 1999 the Kazakh government passed a law requiring subsoil users (such as oil companies) to include natural gas utilization projects in their development plans. As a result, in 2000, Kazakhstan increased its natural gas production to 314 billion cubic feet (Bcf), the highest level in the past decade. According to preliminary 2001 figures, Kazakhstan produced 324 Bcf of natural gas in 2001, a 3.1% increase over 2000. From January 2002 through May 2002, Kazakh natural gas production totaled 158.5 Bcf, a 2.1% year-on-year increase from the

Figure 3-6: Natural Gas Production by Regions in 1993-1999

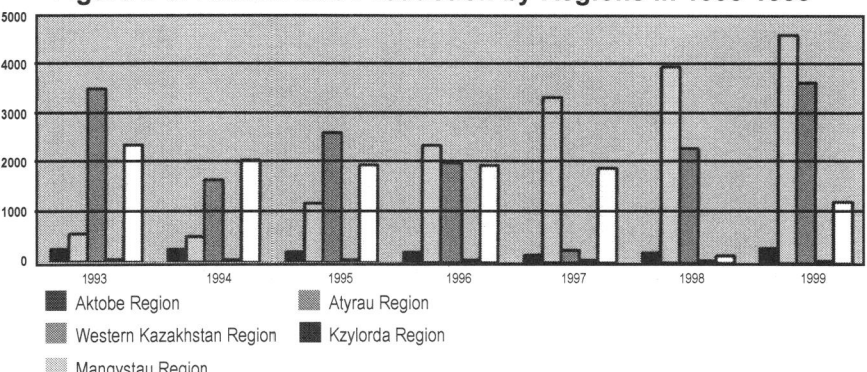

Sources: "Industry of Republic of Kazakhstan. Statistics for 1990-1997." "Industry of the Republic of Kazakhstan and Regions. Statistics for 1990-1998." "Social and Economic Situation in the Republic of Kazakhstan. Jan.-Dec. 1999."

same time period in 2001. At present the country is fulfilling an ambitious strategy of increasing oil production, following with associated natural gas production that will grow by a factor of 2 or 3 by 2010 (this figure is given for Karachaganak and Tengiz only, and does not include other fields). With the existing situation in the gas production infrastructure, tens of billions of cu m of gas may be lost in flares (see Figure 3-6).

Although the international consortium developing Karachaganak is concentrated mainly on producing gas condensate thus far (initially, Karachaganak was opened as an oil deposit, and the international consortium was created for extraction of oil mainly), the field yielded 132 Bcf of natural gas in 2001. Through the first five months of 2002, the Karachaganak Integrated Organization extracted an additional 68.8 Bcf of natural gas from the field (See Figure 3-4).

Figure 3-7: Gas Production by Region, 2000

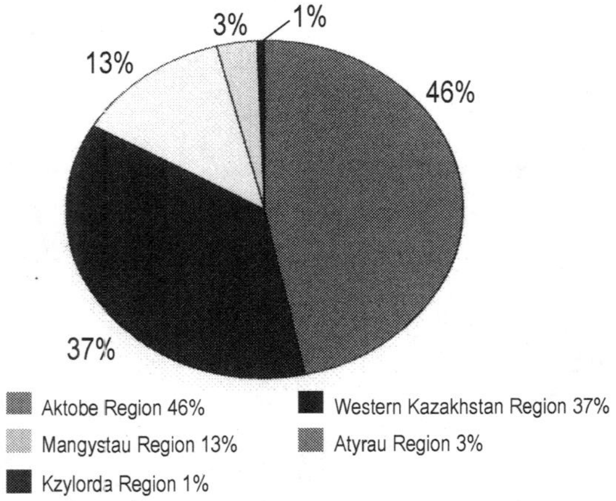

Aktobe Region 46% Western Kazakhstan Region 37%
Mangystau Region 13% Atyrau Region 3%
Kzylorda Region 1%

Source: Kazakhstan State Agency on Statistics and Analysis

Since the signing of the FPSA, Karachaganak has seen dramatic changes. Major refurbishment of the existing production plant has allowed exports of both condensate and gas to reach record levels, and development of the new production and processing facilities is moving on at a good pace. Natural gas together with oil is an important constituent of the GDP. Figure 3-5 illustrates gas production rates in comparison with other products.

Kazakhstan's GDP growth, coming on top of 13.2% expansion in 2002 and 9.8% in 2001, is partially credited by local and international experts to the continuing strong showing of the economy due both to the Government's bold reforms in key economic areas, and to the favorable situation in the commodities markets (increase in the world oil prices).

Despite the fact that gas production exceeds consumption in Kazakhstan (Figure 3-8 shows historical production and consumption in Kazakhstan), shortages do occur in the south of the country. This is because of the fact that the southern regions of Kazakhstan (Almaty, Jambyl, Shymkent oblasts), which have the highest consumption, can technically receive gas only from the territory of neighboring countries, and they have to buy gas at $45-50 plus 16% VAT a thousand cubic meters, which is 2-3 times higher than internal prices. Figures 3-6 and 3-7 show natural gas production by various regions of Kazakhstan. The five gas producing regions have a low population density and a low consumption rate, while the southern regions do not produce gas, which could become a reliable supply base for industries and households. The southern regions under the full load of industrial enterprises have a consumption rate up to 3 bln cu m of gas monthly.

A fall in consumption and exports in 1998 was accompanied by a rise in the production of gas and this all was at the time of the lowest oil and gas prices in the world markets. This best illustrates the poor management of the gas industry in Kazakhstan (See Figure 8). In 2001 production still highly exceeded consumption, while export options and storage facilities had not yet been developed. Overproduction of gas is projected to increase up to 13 bln cu m in 2005, 24 bln cu m in 2010 and 34 bln cu m in 2015.

The privatization of the gas-distribution networks in regions was very difficult. This was even more evident against the background of compa-

Figure 3-8
Historical Overview of Exports, Imports, Consumption, and Production of Natural Gas in Kazakhstan

Natural Gas, million cubic meters	1989	1990	1992	1994	1995	1996	1997	1998	1999	2000	2001
Exports	...	4200	3915	3451	1636	2566	2342	2432	2306	4245	5221	5539
Imports	...	12800	13400	9772	7173	9121	5495	3004	3052	2783	4218	4880
Consumption	...	16500	17600	14700	10155	11513	11581	11016	4772	5155	5525	7212
Production	...	7885	8113	8685	4488	5916	6524	8114	7948	9946	11542	11572

Source: Kazakhstan State Committee on Statistics and Analysis

nies producing condensed gas, which managed to restore their pre-crisis condition without any sound investment, thanks to their autonomy. This

34

seemed by a large extent to be explained by the fact that all condensed gas enterprises were privatized by domestic private companies in 1996-1997.

The most acute problem is traditionally the ineffective management of the main gas transportation system, which requires considerable funds for the day-to-day management and maintenance of the networks, and their development. The State Kazakhgas Company failed to resolve the

Figure 3-9
Year 2000 Exports

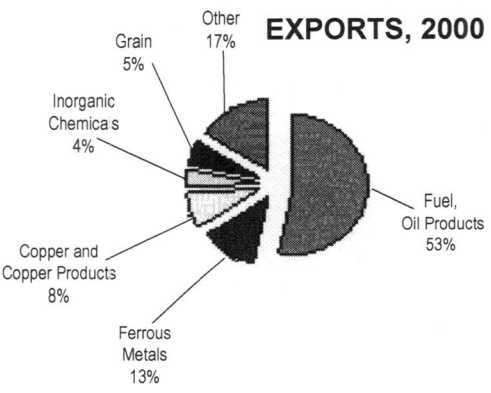

(US$ million)	1999	% of total	2000	% of total
Fuel, oil products	2287.8	40.9	4826.7	52.8
Ferrous Metals	885.6	15.8	1178.3	12.9
Copper and Copper Procucts	575.9	10.3	737.6	8.1
Inorganic Chemicals	323.2	5.8	383.5	4.2
Grain	313.6	5.6	500.5	5.5
CIS countries	1461.4	26.1	2390.4	26.2
Other countries	4130.6	73.9	6749.1	73.8

Source: Committee on Statistics and Analysis

problems of the gas transportation systems and in 1997 Kazakhstan's government transferred control to Tractebel S.A. (Belgium) under a 15-year concession agreement. The concession was given 10 main gas pipelines, 21 compressor stations with pumping facilities, the largest being the Bazoiskoye facility with a capacity of 19 mln cu m. Tractebel failed to comply with the terms of the agreement, which was terminated in 2000, and the assets were transferred to KazTransGas, KazTransOil's subsidiary (which is also a subsidiary of KazMunaiGas at the present time).

Kazmunaigaz, the new state oil and natural gas company, is now the operator of Kazakhstan's main natural gas pipelines. The company, which took over the assets of KazTransGaz when it was created in February

Figure 3-10
Year 2000 Imports

IMPORTS, 2000

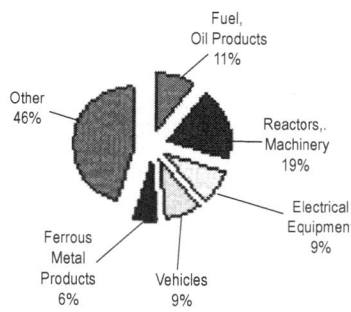

(US$ million)	1999	% of total	2000	% of total
Fuel, oil products	341.0	9.3	572	11.3
Reactors, machinery	661.1	18.0	947.7	18.8
Electrical equipment	308.1	8.4	443.6	8.8
Vehicles	356.7	9.7	441.6	8.7
Ferrous metal products	220.6	6.0	321.2	6.4
CIS countries	1594.4	43.3	2757.3	54.6
Other countries	2088.4	56.7	2294.8	45.4

Source: Committee on Statistics and Analysis

2002, owns over 5,400 miles of trunk pipelines, as well as 26 compressor stations with 308 gas transportation units. Since Kazakhstan is such a large, sparsely populated country, it has two separate domestic natural gas distribution networks, in the west and in the south.

However, due to the lack of a pipeline linking the natural gas fields in the western part of the country to consumers in the south, the southern areas of Kazakhstan are almost completely dependent on imported supplies (See Figure 3-10). Although Kazakhstan is considering the construction of an internal pipeline to link its natural gas-producing and consuming areas, the prohibitive cost (at least $1 billion) of such a pipeline has delayed any decision to go ahead with the project.

Kazakhstan invested around $120 million to upgrade its natural gas pipeline network in 2001, including about $10 million for regional systems, regular maintenance, personnel training, and new equipment.

Figure 3-11
Foreign Investments in Kazakhstan's Oil and Gas Industry

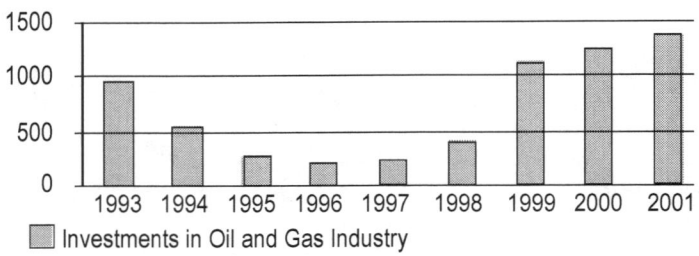

Source: Kazakhstan State Committee on Statistics and Analysis

KazTransGaz began restoration work on the southern natural gas pipeline system in 2001, including repairing 24 miles of pipelines and modernizing 23 wells at the Poltoraskoye underground natural gas storage facility.

Kazakhstan's oil and gas sector still remains one of the most attractive areas of the economy for foreign direct investments. Figure 3-11 represents

Figure 3-12
Foreign Direct Investments in Kazakhstan's
Oil and Gas Industry by Country in 2000

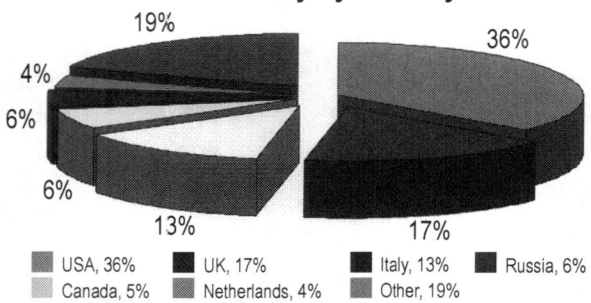

Source: Kazakhstan State Agency on Statistics

the dynamics of the FDI inflow in the oil and gas industry of Kazakhstan. Between 1993 and 1998, Kazakhstan's foreign direct investment (FDI) was $7.9 bln and was concentrated mainly in the areas of oil and gas, electrical utilities, and minerals. FDI peaked in 1997 at $2.1 bln, followed by $1.2 bln predicted in 1998 (See Figure 3-11). At mid-year 1999, FDI was $460 mln with $1.2 bln predicted for the year. Oil and gas attracted 47% of all the cumulative investments in the five-year period. Foreign capital has been attracted to 27 large projects that are related to the development, exploration, and transportation of oil and gas, and the reconstruction of refining enterprises.

Kazakhstan received over US $2.751 bln in foreign direct investments in the year 2000, 48.7% more than in 1999 and twice the amount of investments in 1998, according to figures released by the National Statistics Agency (See Figure 3-12).

Roughly a third of the investment, US $993.4 bln, was received from US-based investors, while British and Italian companies invested US $462.2 mln and US $351 mln in 2001, respectively. These largest investing countries were followed by Russia, whose firms spent US $163.2 mln in Kazakhstan, Canada at US $144.9 mln, and the Netherlands with US $109.9 mln in investments.

The gas transport company KazTransGas has started developing the new Amangeldy gas field (AGF). The Amangeldy field is located in the south of Kazakhstan, 160 km from Taraz city. Preliminary estimates of AGF reserves are about 25 bln cu m of gas. The field is thought to be capable of at least 12-13 years of profitable production.

The field is in a good location. The development of the field will allow energy independence in the region of Southern Kazakhstan, the most densely populated region of the country, through the connection of the new AmangeldyTaraz main gas pipeline to the Gazil-Almaty network. Existing power transmission lines and a motorway to the field will reduce the cost of the project; however, if the Uzbekistan government followed a consistent and fair price policy for gas, it would be easier for Kazakhstan to continue to purchase Uzbek gas, rather than developing a new field. Today the government remains the first and only investor in the AGF. The current situation in the gas industry is full of challenges. Inconsistency between the goals and the strategies is evident. Setting targets of high production growth for the industry along with measures of attracting foreign direct investments, the management of the industry fails to introduce a viable marketing strategy. All this is complicated by the intricate entanglement of politics and the energy industry. Kazakhstan is a potential competitor for Russia, which has immense control over Kazakhstan's exports of natural gas.

Success in achieving higher output of gas, observed during the period of 1999-2002, has brought no real benefits either for the industry or for the country. The tremendous potential of Kazakhstan's gas sector both on the international and domestic markets has been wasted by low quotas granted by Russia and the undeveloped pipeline infrastructure.

Development of the new gas deposit in southern Kazakhstan's Amangeldy field has started to bring positive feedback from the investment, but again, lack of investment and poor strategy towards FDI attraction hinders the development of alternative projects for import substitution.

Gas Industry's Current Objectives, Strategies, and Policies

Kazakhstan's gas industry has four main objectives:

First is steady growth. Kazakhstan plans to enter the top ten of the 98 oil and gas producing countries in the world. Kazakhstan is targeting to become a major exporter of natural gas. Kazakh officials hope to become independent of Uzbek natural gas supplies by 2010. In August 2001, the Kazakh Ministry for Energy and Mineral Resources approved a 15-year strategy for developing the country's natural gas sector that would increase natural gas production fivefold. According to the strategy, which the Kazakh government approved, Kazakhstan is aiming to increase its natural gas production to 1.2 Tcf by 2015, to 1.66 Tcf by 2020, and to 1.84 Tcf by 2030. Key to this strategy is the development of natural gas reserves at Kashagan, Karachaganak, and Tengiz. The growth should be supported by the three other objectives.

Second is the gas industry's infrastructure and gas processing development. Since Kazakh natural gas is a potential competitor with Russian natural gas, several new natural gas export pipelines from the Caspian Sea region also are in development or under consideration, potentially opening up new markets for Kazakh natural gas. In the meantime, Kazakhstan serves as an important natural gas transit center for Turkmen and Uzbek natural gas that is piped to Russia and beyond.

Third is attaining independence from the gas imports of neighboring countries. The southern regions of Kazakhstan will be supplied from the Amangeldy gas deposit and the Ayrykty gas fields in the southern part of the country.

Fourth is becoming independent from Russia on gas exports. With domestic natural gas demand expected to remain stable, Kazakhstan will be able to increase its natural gas exports to nearly 1.2 Tcf by 2015, according to Uzakbai Karabalin, new President of Kazmunaigaz. In June 2002, Kazmunaigaz and Russia's Gazprom created KazRosGaz, a joint venture that will allow Kazakhstan to pipe its natural gas through the Russian pipeline system for the first time. According to Russian officials, KazRosGaz will have the ability to transport 125 billion cubic feet of Kazakh natural gas via Russia which can be increased to 1.77 trillion cubic feet in the future.

Policies and Strategies of the Gas Industry

Kazakhstan is shifting its trade and energy patterns from the former Soviet Union and towards its neighbors in Central Asia, the Caucasus, and Turkey. The TRACECA Program (Transport System Europe-Caucasus-Asia) is developing an East-West corridor from Central Asia, through the Caucasus, across the Black Sea to Europe. This program, which was set up at the European Union Conference in 1993, is often called "the Great Silk Road."

In January 2001, President Nursultan Nazarbayev set up a National Fund to try to level off the effect of fluctuations of oil revenue on the economy. Chevron-Texaco paid $660 mln for a 5% stake in a joint venture in the Tengiz oil field, and that money was designated to go into the

National Fund. Other revenues, such as taxes from oil and gas companies, royalty payments by joint venture partners, and signing bonuses, will also be designated for the National Fund.

In 1997, the government of Kazakhstan issued a decree on privatization and restructuring in the energy sector. Through this decree, all companies in the energy sector have gone through an incorporation process and are legally prepared for future privatization and restructuring. The privatization was painful and slow and resulted in the fact that the President still keeps tight control on the sector, as he has the authority of appointing the presidents of both national operators, KazMunaiGas and its subsidiary KazTransGas.

The government has issued decrees on bankruptcy, taxes, customs, stock exchanges, land, accounting and natural resources. The general trend in Kazakhstan is to deal more with the West and less with the countries of the former Soviet Union.

The Role of KazMunaiGas and KazTransGas in the Management of the Industry

In February 2002, a presidential decree merged the state oil company Kazkhoil (100% State-Owned) and the national oil and gas transportation firm KazTransGaz. The new combined company is called KazMunaiGas.

Until 2000, the country's gas distribution network was operated by the Belgian company Tractebel. This company (or more precisely its subsidiary Almaty Power Consolidated) managed the power facilities in the city of Almaty and in the Almaty region. Tractebel terminated its business in Kazakhstan, and the government transferred its shares to KazTransGas. The company has already become the major stockholder in the Almaty power system. After Tractebel's withdrawal from Kazakhstan, KazTransGas became a 100% owner of the Intergas International transport company.

KazTransGas, the state-owned gas transport company, has established a new holding company to manage the company's expanding assets. Founded in 2000, KazTransGas manages all three of Kazakhstan's mainline gas pipelines with a combined length of 9,000 km. It has been confirmed

Figure 3-13:
Major Projects in the Oil and Gas Industry of Kazakhstan

NAME OF FIELD/ PROJECT	ESTIMATED RESERVES	PROJECTED INVESTMENT	PROJECT STATUS
Aktobe	1 billion barrels of oil	$4.1 billion	Producing 82,707 bbl/d of oil (end-May 2002); produced 8.8 Bcf of natural gas thru first 5 months of 2002
Arman	Unavailable	Unavailable	Produced 6,000 bbl/d of oil in 2001
Emba	Unavailable	Unavailable	Producing 49,500 bbl/d of oil (end-May 2002); produced 1.5 Bcf of natural gas thru first five months of 2002
Hurricane-Kumkol	442 million barrels of crude oil; 67.9 billion cubic feet (Bcf) of natural gas	Unavailable	Producing 87,671 bbl/d of oil (end-May 2002); produced 1 Bcf of natural gas thru first five months of 2002
Karachaganak	2.3 billion recoverable barrels of oil & gas condensate reserves; 16 Tcf of recoverable natural gas reserves	$4 billion for Phase II	Producing 99,865 bbl/d of gas condensate (end-May 2002); produced 68.8 Bcf of natural gas thru first five months of 2002
Karazhan basmunai	Unavailable	Unavailable	Produced 10,300 bbl/d (8/98)
Kashagan	Approximately 40 billion barrels (up to 10 billion of which are thought to be recoverable)	Over $600 million spent since 1993	Second successful well (Kashagan West 1) drilled (3/01); exploration continuing, production by 2005
Kazgermunai	100 million barrels of oil	$300 million	Produced 1,170 bbl/d (8/98)
Kumkol-LUKOIL	Over 600 million barrels of oil	Unavailable	Produced 17,010 bbl/d (8/98)
Kurmangazy	Unavailable	Unavailable	Russia and Kazakhstan recently agreed on a plan to develop jointly the disputed field
Mangistau	Unavailable	Unavailable	Producing 89,551bbl/d of oil (end-May 2002); produced 2.4 Bcf of natural gas thru first five months of 2002
Matin	102 million barrels of oil	Unavailable	Producing 4,011 bbl/d (4/01)
North Buzachi	1 to 1.5 billion barrels of oil	Over $800 million	Development North Buzachi; 3rd test well drilled
Tengiz	6 to 9 billion barrels of oil	$20 billion over 40 years	Producing 253,182 bbl/d of oil (end-May 2002); peak production of 750,000 bbl/d by 2010; produced 56 Bcf of natural gas thru first five months of 2002
Tengiz-Novorossiisk Oil Pipeline	990 mile oil pipeline from Tengiz oil field in Kazakhstan to Russia's Black Sea port of Novorossiisk; Phase I capacity: 565,000bbl/d; Phase II capacity; 1.34 million bbl/d (2015)	$2.6 billion for Phase I; $4.2 billion total when completed	First tanker loaded in Novorossisk (10/01); exported 240,000 bbl/d in April 2002, volumes rising to 400,000 bbl/d by end-2002
Uzen	1.5 billion barrels of oil		Producing 94,467 1bbl/d of oil (end-May 2002); produced 17.8 Bcf of natural gas thru first five months of 2002

that KazTransGas will remain in state hands, while its numerous affiliates might be allowed to attract capital by issuing bonds and other securities. The decision power of this level always has been in the hands of the President and the government. Frequent changes in the top management of the state oil and gas company have been the result of the fight between the too "self-sustainable" management and the government. The president and the government have won this fight.

Figure 3-13 shows the largest projects in the oil and gas industry, major companies involved in the industry and the amount of investment planned.

There are three main producers of gas in the country: Karachaganakgazprom–the largest project–(restructured to JV Karachaganak Petroleum Operating Co), Uzenmunaigaz Production Association and TengizChevroil JV. Out of nine producing enterprises, three companies are KazMunaiGas subsidiaries (including Uzenmunaigaz). The company also maintains interests in other enterprises (including TengizChevroil). Gas fields are also developed by Kazmunaigas. Karachaganak Integrated Organization was created by four companies Agip (ENI) – 32, 5%; British Gas – 32, 5%, LUKOIL – 15% and Texaco – 20%.

The Karachaganak field, discovered in 1979, is one of the world's largest oil and gas/condensate fields. Located in northwest Kazakhstan, it holds reserves of over 2.4 billion bbls of condensate and more than 16 tcf of gas, recoverable over the 40-year license period. Production from the field began in 1984. Currently all condensate and gas produced from the field is processed at the Orenburg facility in Russia. In 1992, to stimulate further field development, the Kazakh authorities granted BG and Agip exclusive rights to negotiate a preliminary Production Sharing Agreement (PSA). In 1995, a Production Sharing Principles Agreement (PSPA) was signed, under which BG, Agip and Gazprom, who had been brought into the group, took over operations of the field in order to both, halt rapid production decline, and improve the safety and environmental performance of the facilities. Texaco (now ChevronTexaco) acquired a 20% share of Karachaganak from BG and Agip in August 1997, and two months later

LUKOIL took over the 15% share of the project formerly held by Gazprom. In 2001, the BG share of sales of liquids and gas from Karachaganak was 16 mmboe, compared with 18 mmboe in 2000 and 13 mmboe in 1999. In April 2002, KIO set a new daily record of 16,376 tons of condensate exported to Orenburg. The gas produced will be either sold into the Russian market or reinvested into the reservoir.

British Gas, UK

BG plc subsidiary, BG Exploration and Production Ltd. has signed production sharing agreements paving the way for the undertaking of two major ventures in Kazakhstan. The ventures came under the agreements for development of the giant Karachaganak oil and gas field in western Kazakhstan and, in a different partnership, for exploration rights for the Kazakh sector of the Caspian. These agreements represented an important step forward for BG. The Karachaganak agreement gave BG a leading role in one of the world's largest oil and gas fields, and may be substantially larger than any North Sea discovery. Karachaganak is a major development and an important part of BG plans for increasing production from 150,000 to 400,000 barrels of oil equivalent per day, projected for 2015.

BG's share of the development costs of the Karachaganak field following the PSA is around £400 million. Further phases of the development still to be detailed envisage production levels up to 260,000 barrels of oil per day and 1.4 billion cubic feet of gas per day. BG first came to Kazakhstan at the very beginning of the 1990s. It is one of the largest foreign investors in the country.

British Gas's movement was towards concentration solely on the development of the Kazarachaganak oil and gas deposit. On March 7, 2003, BG announced the sale of an 8.33 percent stake in Kazakhstan North Caspian Operating Company (NCOC) to the China National Offshore Oil Corporation for $615 mln. The company's participation in Kazakhstan is currently limited to 32.5 percent stake in the consortium to develop Karachaganak gas field, and a 2 percent stake in the Caspian Pipeline Consortium.

ENI (Agip), Italy

ENI was one of the first western companies to begin exploration and production activities in Kazakhstan and is currently involved in three big projects: the development of the gas and condensate fields in Karachaganak, the development of the northern area of the Caspian Sea and the construction of an oil pipeline that will link Kazakhstan to the Black Sea.

ENI operates in Kazakhstan in the exploration and production of hydrocarbons, the distribution of oil products and in engineering and oil-field services. The first concerns the further development of oil, gas, and condensate reserves in Karachaganak, already operative from the nineties, in northwest Kazakhstan. ENI, with a 32.5% stake, is co-operator together with British Gas. Planned investments come to $4.9 billion ($1.6 for ENI). The development plan has been organized in three phases.

The first, already completed, concerned the maintenance of the wells and plant at the field. In 2002, daily production of condensates and natural gas for ENI came to 32,000 and 25,500 boe respectively. For the time being, the production is sold in the Russian Federation through Orenburg.

The second development phase of the field has the target to further increase, within 2005, the production of the field with a daily production for ENI's quota equal to 62,000 barrels of condensates and 35,000 boe of gas. The achievement of a production peak of 72,000 barrels of liquids for ENI's quota is foreseen for 2009. For the transportation of the liquids, the KIO consortium has already built a 460-km pipeline from Bolshoy Chagan, located 190 km from the Karachaganak field, to Atyrau on the coast of the Caspian Sea in northern Kazakhstan. The first oil will be sent through the CPC as of summer 2003.

The second project concerns the exploration and development of an offshore area in southern Kazakhstan's Caspian Sea southeast of Atyrau. The project, known as the North Caspian Sea Project, is carried out by a consortium made up of ENI (through Agip Caspian Sea B.V., with a 16.67% stake), and six other international oil companies.

In February 2001, ENI was nominated single operator in the production sharing agreement for the North Caspian Sea Project. ENI established a company (wholly-owned by Agip Caspian Sea B.V.), in the context of the production sharing agreement, known as Agip Kazakhstan North Caspian Operating Company N.V. (Agip KCO) that operates on behalf of the consortium. Exploration activities are currently underway. In 2000, an important discovery was made at the KE-1 exploration well in the Kashagan structure. The importance of the discovery was confirmed by a successive exploration well, KW-1, 40 km from the first and by the subsequent appraisal activities. In June 2002, the joint venture and Kazakhstan's State Company, KazMunaiGaz, declared the "Commercial Discovery" of Kashagan. In the North Caspian Sea PSA, besides Kashagan there exist other high potential structures. In August 2002, the Kalamkas-1 well was drilled, which made a discovery in a block of southern Kashagan. ENI has promised production to start by the end of 2005, although full capacity will probably not be reached before 2010.

The topic of the withdrawal of hydrocarbons produced in Kazakhstan represents a major priority for the country that needs big transportation infrastructures. In this sector, ENI is part of the Caspian Pipeline Consortium (CPC) that, in 2001, activated the maxi-oil pipeline with the actual capacity of 28 million tons per year, which makes it possible to transport crude oil from the Tengiz field—close to the Caspian Sea—to the Russian port of Novorossisk on the Black Sea. This involvement will allow ENI to market around 3 million tons of the oil production from Karachaganak per year. In the future CPC, in its final configuration, will allow transporting 67 million t/y of crude oil. ENI also expects to extend this pipe through an agreement pending with Gasprom to build a pipeline connecting Turkey and Russia through the Black Sea.

ENI has been present since 1998 with a service station in the new capital, Astana. Through Saipem, world leader in onshore and offshore oilfield work, ENI is actively involved in the Karachaganak project in the engineering and oilfield services sector. In association with Consolidated Contractors International Co. (CCC), the company is developing civil engineering, infrastructure, and mechanical works for a production unit, a gas re-injection plant, a process plant, and a 635 km-long pipeline with a pumping station and terminal for the development of the large oilfield of Karachaganak.

ChevronTexaco, USA

ChevronTexaco extracts 12.5 million tons of oil annually in Kazakhstan. Up to now ChevronTexaco has invested about $4 billion in the development of some Kazakh oilfields—Tengiz, Karachaganak, and North Buzachi.

The new 900-mile Caspian pipeline connects western Kazakhstan to Novorossiysk on the Russian Black Sea coast and allows for maximum development of the Tengiz field. ChevronTexaco is the largest oil company member of the Caspian Pipeline Consortium.

Production at Kazakhstan's biggest oilfield run by a ChevronTexaco-led consortium has created a 35-foot-tall (11 meter) slab of yellow sulfur next to the field's pipelines and storage tanks impacting the health of workers and people living near the operation. The sulfur is a byproduct of poisonous hydrogen sulfide gas found along with the oil that is pumped at Tengiz, a semi-desert environment where this former part of the Soviet Union meets the Caspian Sea in Central Asia.

LUKOIL, Russia

LUKOIL is currently participating in the implementation of three Kazakh oil and gas projects: namely, the development of the major West-Kazakh fields of Tengiz (as a member of the international TengizChevroil consortium) and Karachaganak (as a member of the KIO consortium); and development of the Kumkol field (Kyzyl-Ordin Region, central Kazakhstan) within the framework of the Russo-Canadian Turgai Petroleum joint venture.

LUKOIL, via joint venture with Atlantic Richfield Company (USA), owns a 12.5%-stake in the Caspian Pipeline Consortium, and owns a 5%-interest in a consortium to develop the Tengiz oilfield in Kazakhstan.

Figure 3-14:
Worldwide Gas Conumption
by Regions in 1999

Middle East	7.6%
Africa	2.3%
Asia-Pacific	11.7%
North America	31.6%
South America	4.0%
Europe	19.4%
Former USSR	23.4%

Source: Adapted from National Statistics Agency
of Kazakhstan

Field developments will be matched by investment in major transportation systems, either liquefied natural gas (LNG) or pipeline, in regions such as SE Asia, South America and linking Central Asia / Middle East to Europe.

The three largest gas markets in the world are: *North America*, where the main market is the USA, *Europe,* and the former *Soviet Union.* Due to gas transportation features, the markets in Europe and North America have little connection. Gas production in the United States is located in the southern states near the Gulf of Mexico and in the middle states. The USA also imports gas from Canada, where the gas fields are situated in the western provinces. In 1999 the USA imported about 15.3 percent of utilized gas. The main European gas fields are located on the shelf of the North Sea. Therefore, the main European oil-production countries are those that have an outlet to the sea (See Figure 3-14).

Europe also imports gas from Algeria (about 7.4 percent in 1999) and from Russia (28.3 percent). The large gas consumption in the countries of the former Soviet Union is due to the structure of the industry inherited from the USSR, which relied heavily on the cheap source of energy abundant in the country. For comparison, gas share in the energy balance of the CIS countries is above 50 percent, but for the United States the share is about 25 percent and for European countries it is about 22 percent.

Gas in the world is distributed less equally than oil. As we can see from the diagrams (Figures 3-14 & 3-15), the share of North America in production and consumption is almost the same. It means that the region provides itself with gas completely. But for Europe the share of gas production is less than the share of gas consumption. The third diagram seems the most interesting. As we can see, above 70 percent of the world's proven gas reserves are located in two regions, namely in the former Soviet Union and in the Middle East. Moreover, Russia and Iran possess almost half of the proven gas reserves.

World gas consumption is expected to rise. According to the Energy Information Administration, gas demand will reach above 4000 billion cubic meters in 2015. The highest growth rates in natural gas demand are projected for the developing countries where overall demand will be about 5 percent annually. Southeast Asia is expected to experience annual gas consumption increases of almost 8 percent. The electricity industry will make the largest contribution in overall gas demand.

Among industrialized regions, Western Europe is projected to have

Figure 3-15:
Worldwide Gas Production
by Regions in 1999

Middle East	8.0%
Africa	5.9%
Asia-Pacific	9.9%
North America	31.8%
South America	4.1%
Europe	12.1%
Former USSR	28.2%

Source: Adapted from National Statistics Agency
of Kazakhstan

Figure 3-16
Gas Consumption by Sectors
in Kazakhstan, 2002

Industry	70%
Agriculture	1%
Construction	10%
Transport	16%
Trade & Food Industry	1%
Household & Utilities	1%
Others	1%

Source: Adapted from National Statistics Agency
of Kazakhstan

the highest growth rate in gas use, at 3.8 percent. The privatization and restructuring of the electric utility sector in many countries of the region have resulted in plans to increase the use of natural gas for generating electricity. Further, many nations of Western Europe see the use of natural gas as a way to decrease greenhouse gas emissions. European governments are encouraging the development of gas infrastructure in an attempt to move away from reliance on the more carbon-intensive coal and oil.

New gas field discoveries take place every year and the technique of gas exploration is improved constantly. Also it is necessary to say something about the remote future of gas exploration. Immense amounts of methane naturally occur in gas hydrate deposits located in oceanic sediments and in sediments underlying the Arctic permafrost zone. These deposits constitute by far the largest potentially available source of methane on Earth. Worldwide, the amount of carbon in gas hydrates is conservatively estimated to be twice the amount that is believed to exist in all other fossil fuel on Earth. The total methane volume resident in gas hydrates is in the range of from 385 to 945 trillion cubic meters. Japan has a $50 million program in place and plans to demonstrate the industrial use of hydrates. Norway also has a methane hydrate research program.

Kazakhstan sees Russia, Eastern and Western Europe as well as the Asian Pacific region as the most attractive markets for its gas exports. Kazakhstan's domestic market for gas is different from the international one, because on the second level of the structure (the distributor), there is a single company, and there is actually no free market for gas in Kazakhstan. The main end users of gas are shown in Figure 3-16.

The main distributor of gas is Kazmunaigaz, which is a relatively new state oil and natural gas company, and now the operator of Kazakhstan's main natural gas pipelines. The company, which took over the assets of KazTransGaz when it was created in February 2002, owns over 5,400 miles of trunk pipelines, as well as 26 compressor stations with 308 gas transportation units. Since Kazakhstan is such a large, sparsely populated country, it has two separate domestic natural gas distribution networks, in the west and in the south.

However, due to the lack of a pipeline linking the natural gas fields in the western part of the country to consumers in the south, the southern areas of Kazakhstan are almost completely dependent on imported supplies. Although Kazakhstan is considering the construction of an internal pipeline to link its natural gas producing and consuming areas, the prohibitive cost (at least $1 billion) of such a pipeline has delayed any decision to go ahead with the project.

Kazakhstan invested around $120 million to upgrade its natural gas pipeline network in 2001, including about $10 million in meters for regional systems, regular maintenance, personnel training, and new equipment. KazTransGaz began restoration work on the southern natural gas pipeline system in 2001, including repairing 24 miles of pipelines and modernizing 23 wells at the Poltoraskoye underground natural gas storage facility.

In the distribution aspect, the Kazakhstan government and all the companies—players of the industry—do everything possible to diminish the dependence of Kazakhstan's oil and gas exports on Russia.

Natural Gas Export Options

Although Kazakhstan is currently a net importer of natural gas, with the expected increase in the country's natural gas production, Kazakh officials project that the country's natural gas exports could reach 1.2 trillion cubic feet (Tcf) per year by 2015. However, Kazakhstan's natural gas-producing areas are not linked to its internal pipeline network, and the country suffers from a lack of export infrastructure. In order to reach its natural gas exporting potential, therefore, Kazakhstan must either negotiate to export via the Russian natural gas pipeline system or develop new ways of getting its natural gas to customers.

In June 2002, Kazakhstan's Kazmunaigaz and Russia's natural gas monopoly Gazprom announced the formation of a joint venture, KazRos-Gaz, which will start by transporting 124 billion cubic feet (Bcf) of natural gas through the Russian pipeline system, with volumes rising as Kazakh natural gas production increases. The deal will allow Kazakhstan to receive access to the Russian pipeline system, where previously Kazakhstan had to sell its natural gas on the border with Russia.

Natural Gas Transit

Kazakhstan already is a transit route for natural gas from Turkmenistan and Uzbekistan flowing to Russia and on to other markets in the former Soviet Union via the Central Asia-Center Pipeline and the Bukhara-Urals Pipeline. In addition, Russian natural gas flowing westward crosses into Kazakh territory in the northwest of the country. Kazakhstan earns approximately $400 million per year from natural gas transit fees.

The majority of Turkmen and Uzbek natural gas that transits Kazakhstan is pumped north along the Central Asia-Center natural gas pipeline. However, deterioration of compressor stations and various stretches of the pipeline have eroded the pipeline system's 3.53 Tcf per year capacity: according to Turkmen officials, capacity on the Central Asia-Center pipeline is only about 2.4 Tcf to 2.5 Tcf presently due to a lack of maintenance and repair.

With Turkmen and Uzbek planning to increase natural gas exports via Kazakhstan, the Bukhara-Urals pipeline has been pressed into service. In March 2001, natural gas transit started on the previously inactive pipeline, with approximately 200 Bcf exported via the pipeline in 2001. Kazakhstan invested about $20 million in modernizing its section of the Bukhara-Urals pipeline system in 2000.

Kazakhstan needs about $360 million to restore its section of the Central Asia-Center pipeline to enable the country to handle the increased transit volumes from Turkmenistan and Uzbekistan. Increased capacity on the pipeline also will be necessary for Kazakhstan to export its own natural gas from Kashagan and Karachaganak. The country should develop its infrastructure to meet domestic demand and concentrate on the development of the new Amangeldy deposit, which also can be a source for Kazakhstan's neighbors in the East.

The most feasible alternative strategy for the industry is development of the Amangeldy gas deposit. According to independent experts, the total amount required to finance the development of the entire group of fields may come to US $700-750 mln. For the first phase, the development will minimally cost US $76.7 mln. This amount includes construction of the gas pipeline (US $36.7 mln), drilling and servicing wells (US $21 mln), construction of a gas processing plant (US $10 mln) and miscellaneous expenses (US $9 mln). The second phase may require US $258 mln. This includes further development of the field. ABN AMRO Bank, Citibank, Islamic Bank of Development as well as some Kazakh banks have expressed interest in development of the field.

Quite important for Kazakhstan's observing international standards and rules of trade is the Republic's entry into the World Trade Organization, which is why in January 1996 an application was submitted for entry into the GATT/WTO. Along with this, measures were taken to bring the national foreign trade legislation into compliance with the WTO principles and standards. They also conducted multilateral and bilateral negotiations with major partner-countries with regard to terms of mutual access to commodities and services and certain activities are on their way to prepare a Memorandum on a foreign trade regime in Kazakhstan.

Taking into account the fact that Kazakhstan is becoming the focus of interest of a number of countries, she can attract them in the development of the pipeline infrastructure. The bright example is that a new project involving Central Asian gas is being developed to supply the European Union. It has been estimated that the EU will increase its natural gas requirement from the current 45% to 59% in the year 2010 and to 77% by the year 2020. Apart from Russia and Algeria (LNG), potential natural gas suppliers for the EU are the Caspian countries Azerbaijan and Kazakhstan and in the long-term future Turkmenistan and Uzbekistan, as well as North African countries like Egypt and Libya. The EU strongly supports the multiplicity of both suppliers and transport pipelines as a means of diversifying its energy supply resources and consequently lowering the prices. As far as Greece and Turkey are concerned, the proposed Karacabey-Komotini gas interconnection represents an alternative supply route to the present one directed to Russia. The proposed new route will facilitate the supply of natural gas from the Shah Deniz field in Azerbaijan and provide Turkey, Greece, and the entire EU with a feasible alternative capable of satisfying the increasing energy demand.

Chapter 4

The Transportation Industry:
Where Modernity
and Mobility Benefit Kazakhstan

Introduction

As in all other sectors of Kazakhstan's industry, the necessary maintenance as well as the updating and upgrading had been neglected under the Soviet administration for a century. Therefore, the need for a considerable size of capital infusion as well as updating of technology is of utmost importance to Kazakhstan.

In recent years, the transport and communication complex has accounted for at least 9.12% of the national GDI. The freight transport system is an essential part of Kazakhstan's economy (See Figures 4-1 & 4-2) because of its large size with a sparse population density of six inhabitants per square kilometer. Not only her population but also her natural resources and the centers of economic activity are widely dispersed. In addition, the remoteness to foreign markets is another disadvantage for the country. And it is a great challenge for this new nation to develop a system whereby she can efficiently and effectively run the entire transportation system to serve her domestic and foreign trade as well.

Some segments of the industry, such as the roads connecting major cities, are in relatively good condition, but all others are in dire need of improvement. Some others, such as national gas pipelines, are even worse because of so many years of neglect and disrepair; hence, it would be better simply to be rebuilt entirely.

With the new emphasis on the production of raw materials and intermediary goods that Kazakhstan now generates, the demand for a large volume of foreign transport is not adequately met by the current condition. The vastness of the land and the lack of an ocean outlet require a better systematic transportation system to meet the contemporary needs. As of now, the cost of transport may account for up to 50 to 90% of the total cost of some important exports, such as grain and coal. One cannot ignore the fact that the cost and quality of transport for internal and external trade affect the efficiency of Kazakhstan's economy.

Passenger transportation is also important in Kazakhstan, though it does not have the same level of intensity as freight transport because of its historical background of the people having been more tribal while scattered than most other societies. Also its harsh climate is not conducive to its population owning private automobiles either.

In 2006, there were 626 support enterprises, of which only 68 were state-owned companies, and the remaining 558 were privately owned. In 2005, freight traffic activities amounted to 320 million tons, their highest level since 1996.

The unsatisfactory performance of urban public transportation and civil aviation are also major concerns for the governance. The national railway system does not offer speed and reliability either. Each year, substantial parts of the road network continue to fall below minimum

Figure 4-1
Major Indicators of Transport Sector Development
(Economic Impact)

	2003	2004	2005	2006
Revenue (million Tenge)	243,499	333,351.8	427,608.9	456,929.5
Gross margin	136,643.4	172,744.9	212,508.4	212,595.3
% Contribution to GDP	9.7	10.3	12.3	10.5

Source: "Transport in the Republic of Kazakhstan," Statistical Data, Almaty, 2007

Figure 4-2
Major Indicators of
Transport Sector Development
(Quantity)

	2002	2003	2004	2005	2006
Freight transported (million tons)					
By railroad	140.2	190.9	170.0	133.7	171.8
By road	39.6	28.9	20.04	19.9	24.3
By pipeline	41.1	79.9	76.8	106.2	138.8
By air	25.5	24.6	14.5	17.2	14.4
By river	1.2	1	0.45	0.181	0.45
Turnover of goods (million tons/kilometer)					
By railroad	112.7	106.4	10.3.0	91.7	125.0
By road	1.3	1.2	0.8	0.89	0.92
By pipeline	22.5	30.9	27.0	34.7	50.9
By air	136.5	77.4	50.8	63.6	117.5
By river	0.4	0.3	0.14	0.025	0.042
Passengers transported (million people)					
By railroad	31.8	27.5	21.6	18.9	21.3
By bus	1209.0	984.3	730.2	542.8	505.7
By car	10.3	9.2	11.9	7.8	7.4
By trolleybus	195.4	176.2	139.4	106.8	81.0
By tram	77.5	65.6	54.5	53.6	70.4
By air	1.5	1.7	1	0.79	0.77
By river	0.4	0.3	0.14	0.069	0.059
Passenger turnover (million per kilometer)					
By railroad	14,188	12,802	10,669	8,859	10,215
By bus	9,506	7,979	6,177	4,588	4,819
By car	120	99	117	61	64
By trolleybus and tram	1,156	1,018	818	675	632
By air	3,308	2,202	2,100	2,136	1,797
By river	6.2	6.4	2.3	0.43	1.07

Source: "Transport in the Republic of Kazakhstan," Statistical Data, Almaty, 2007

quality standards, affecting the reliability of road transport and, ultimately, the development of some of the most dynamic parts of the economy (See Figures 4-1 & 4-2).

Transportation Overview

Since 1991, after her independence, the demand for transport declined [because the materials which were transported to the Soviet Union ceased], and now Kazakhstan finds herself in the situation of having an oversupply of leftover poor-quality assets, while specialized facilities and equipment are in serious shortage. However, during the last four or five years (2003-2007), the republic of Kazakhstan has steadily been improving her transportation infrastructure.

Figure 4-3
Passenger Transportation by Various Modes
(million people)

	2003	2004	2005	2006
International				
By bus	56.5	21.7	16.1	10.5
By railroad	16.4	16.3	14.1	15.4
By air	2	1	0.8	0.4
By river	0.02	n/a	n/a	n/a
Provincial				
By bus	185.6	80.5	37.6	30.8
By railroad	20.9	5.3	4.7	5.8
By river	0.1	0.1	n/a	n/a
By taxi	0.9	0.2	0.1	0.1
Urban				
By bus	1,292.3	628	475.7	459.3
By taxi	13.3	11.7	16.4	7.3
By trolleybus	210.7	139.4	106.8	118.6
By tram	94.4	54.4	53.6	70.4
By river	0.3	0.1	0.1	0.1

Source: "Transport in the Republic of Kazakhstan," Statistical Data, Almaty, Kazakhstan

Rail network: The size of the rail network is generally adequate, and the railways have a large number of locomotives and wagons. There are some important gaps in the network's electrification, however, as well as serious shortages of passenger coaches and some specialized wagons (See Figure 4-3). There are acute problems as to the availability of passenger coaches, and many diesel locomotives are also awaiting repairs; accumulated depreciation for locomotives accounted for 65-70%. In addition, about 30% of the rail network is in need of major repairs.

Airports: Kazakhstan's airlines have lower productivity and higher operating costs than comparable Western airlines. The country's airport facilities are at the level of a typical developing nation:

- Some runways are in need of urgent repairs;
- There is a great need for an air fleet; and
- Only a few planes are currently adapted for international traffic.

According to statistical data, passenger air travel decreased from 1.5 million people in 1996 to 0.77 million people in 2000. Air cargo also decreased during this same period from 25.5 million tons to 14.4 million tons. Since then, however, airline passenger and cargo traffic have increased since 2007, by about 15%.

Ports: Kazakhstan is a land-locked country, and therefore water transportation is only of regional importance. There is only one major port on the Caspian Sea, and Kazakhstan has no sea trade fleet.

Pipelines: There are a limited number of pipelines to transport domestic oil, most of which is extracted in the western part of the country. Overall, the quality of these facilities, equipment, etc., relating to the transportation system in Kazakhstan is a major problem. In most cases, assets are in poor condition, as mentioned earlier, and not adequately maintained. And they are quickly deteriorating. In addition, they are often technologically obsolete, and some of their inherent characteristics, such as size and power, limit their use. Since the country's independence, very little asset renewal has taken place because of the lack of funds. As a result, there is a major problem in both efficiency and, increasingly,

Figure 4-4
Distribution of Cargo Transport Types
(%)

	1995	2000	2005
Pipelines	4	15	25
Auto	10	7	13
Railways	86	78	62
Total	100	100	100

Source: National Statistics Agency of Kazakhstan (2007)

its capacity in the transportation sector. For the future, it is necessary to achieve the means to ensure a low cost of transportation, reliability of the transportation system, its safety, and speed of delivery. Also, the reputation of the transportation system must be maintained and advanced technology, in terms of Information System and equipment, must be safeguarded.

Road network: The road network, comprising 85,867 kilometers, reaches most parts of the country where the population is sufficiently dense. However, road conditions are worsening because there are no funds

Figure 4-5
Transportation of Cargo by Public Railways
(million tons)

	2002	2003	2004	2005	2006
Coal	71,440	69,148	68,442	58,258	74,128
Coke	65	196	86	61	249
Oil and oil products	12,688	13,593	14,309	15,295	17,747
Ore	15,438	19,159	11,320	23,009	29,361
Black metal	3,089	3,864	3,379	4,125	4,735
Crowbar of black metal	686	705	n/a	1,586	2,618
Chemical & mineral fertilizations	3,199	2,123	993	1,301	810
Mineral building cargos	n/a	6,318	7,042	5,577	7,580
Cement	978	501	473	680	967
Wood cargos	185	205	323	401	707
Bread cargos	4,413	5,116	517	4,805	7,339
Other cargos	27,969	15,528	19,069	8,837	10,155
Total	140,150	136,456	129,953	123,935	156,396

Source: National Statistics Agency of Kazakhstan (2007)

for road rehabilitation: about 1,500 kilometers of main roads are being lost each year. Three-quarters of the track fleet are gasoline-powered, and fuel consumption on vehicles is much higher than that of the other developed

Figure 4-6
Operating Length of Public Railways
(kilometers)

	1995	2000	2005
Akhmolinskaya	1,491	1,531	1,648
Akhtubinskaya	1,142	1,148	1,147
Almatinskaya	1,252	1,274	1,125
Atyrauskaya	758	742	751
East-Kazakhstan	1,180	1,175	1,332
Zhambylskaya	1,116	1,064	1,035
West-Kazakhstan	417	417	431
Karagandinskaya	1,867	1,847	1,827
Kostanaiskaya	1,136	1,048	1,182
Kysilardinskaya	760	760	763
Mangistauskaya	776	775	775
Pavlodarskaya	734	733	734
North-Kazakhstan	1,226	1,235	883
South-Kazakhstan	608	609	561
Roads of Republic of Kazakhstan on Territory of other Republics			337
Republic of Kazakhstan – total	14,463	14,358	14,530

Source: National Statistics Agency of Kazakhstan (2007)

nations, wasting energy and contributing to a serious air pollution problem in several cities (including the capital, Astana). Due to the very poor condition and operational performance of urban buses and trolley buses, there is not enough capacity in the major cities to move passengers, or ensure even minimum levels of service quality. The number of passenger cars in 2005 is relatively small, with only about 1 million passenger cars in Kazakhstan (or, 59 cars per 1,000 people; about the same level as in Turkey). Auxiliary services for road transport (fuel supply, service stations, parking facilities) are also in short supply (See Figures 4-4 thru 4-6).

Ground Transportation

Railways: The railway is the basic transport system in Kazakhstan, accounting for more than 85% of the nation's total freight transportation, and 55% of the transportation of passengers. It does offer cheap cargo transportation services to CIS and non-CIS countries.

Being located at the heart of the Eurasian continent, Kazakhstan is a natural transport crossroads. The following transcontinental corridors pass via the territory of Kazakhstan: The Trans-Asian main line–the central direction (Druzhba-Aktogai-Syak-Mointy-Astana-Presnogorkovskaya); the Eurasian main line; the central Asian corridor (Chengeldy-Kandadgach-Ozinki); the western corridor (Aksaraiskaya-Makat-Beineu).

In 2003, there were a total of 825 stations, including 11 merchandising yards, 60 cargo stations, 58 local stations and 696 way stations and halts. Electric traction accounted for 27 percent of the total number of the carriages. There were 2,600 locomotives (diesel and electric locomotives), 93,000 freight cars, and 2,300 passenger cars. In the future, the electrification of up to 50 percent of the densest parts is planned, leading to an increase in the average traveling speed of cargo and passenger trains.

In the past 10 years, the structure of cargo transportation has changed: the share of coal and oil and petroleum products increased from 38 percent and 7.4 percent in 1991, to 47 percent and 11.4 percent in 2005, respectively.

Roads: Freight and passenger transport includes state-owned transport (trucks and automobiles for freight, and municipal buses and trolley buses for passenger transport) and privately-owned transport modes (trucks, auto-freight for freight, and privately-owned buses and taxis for passenger transportation). Domestically, state-owned freight transport is far outweighed by privately-owned freight transport, as the vast majority of motor transportation enterprises have been privatized since 1992.

For both passenger and freight road transport, there are problems with licensing requirements (obligatory licensing for right deliver transportation services–for non-state owned companies) and the absence of adequate technical standards. Another problem is the lack of an appropriate road-user charge policy. In the past, user charges were not directly related to the road wear and tear for which they were responsible. If such a system persists, road transport will not be used as efficiently as it should. In addition, Kazakhstan's road sub-sector suffers from the weakness of the institutions responsible for its management and administration, as well as from the underdevelopment of the country's road construction industry. In these areas, Kazakhstan lags far behind countries such as Russia and the Baltic States.

Transport enterprises and other businesses dealing with commercial freight traffic transported 24.3 million tons of cargo in 2000. Though this number has increased in recent years, the carrying capacity of the motor transport system remains underutilized. In 1999 and 2000, annual freight movement by road declined more than 20 percent per year because of the shift to more efficient means of transport. Sixty percent of cargo vehicles

Figure 4-7:
Length of Highways, by Province
(kilometer)

	2000	2005
Akhmolinskaya	6,286	7,920
Akhtubinskaya	6,143	6,167
Almatinskaya	9,588	9,681
Atyrauskaya	2,987	2,752
East-Kazakhstan	9,890	9,930
Zhambylskaya	5,234	4,104
West-Kazakhstan	5,384	5,353
Karagandinskaya	8,769	8,752
Kostanaiskaya	7,993	8,333
Kysilardinskaya	2,614	2,612
Mangistauskaya	2,543	2,551
Pavlodarskaya	4,922	4,922
North-Kazakhstan	9,781	7,529
South-Kazakhstan	5,203	5,261
Republic of Kazakhstan – total	**87,337**	**85,867**

Source: National Statistics Agency of Kazakhstan (2007)

belong to the private sector. Truck haulage by non-transport organizations and businesses increased by 15.2 percent, while that of haulage contractors by 42.9 percent. Dry products, frozen and refrigerated goods, and mineral oil constitute half of the cargo transported by trucks.

Within the motor sector, during the year 2000, 68 percent of freight is hauled via urban and suburban commercial routes, 29 percent is long-distance, and 3 percent is international. The total length of regular roads is 85,857 kilometers (See Figure 4-7). National roads comprise 17,670 kilometers (60 percent of all motor transport routes). Of these, 11,800 kilometers are regarded as having an international status. Rural roads comprise 69,667 kilometers. There are more than 3,000 bridges and flyovers along the road networks.

The development of road transport in Kazakhstan is challenged by difficult natural and climatic conditions in the regions, as well as a lack of suitable routes out of the country to countries such as China, India, Iran, Pakistan, and Turkey. The development of road facilities requires the creation of high-speed highways with international connections to other CIS countries and further abroad, as well as the reconstruction and strengthening of bridges along strategic routes. In addition to other international donors, the International Bank for Reconstruction and Development has provided $40 million in funding of urban transport projects to improve passenger transport modes in the main cities in the country (Almaty, Karaganda, Shymkent, and Astana).

Water Transportation

Water transportation is the fourth element in the Kazakhstan transport system with both state and private companies operating in this field. The length of water routes is around 6,000 kilometers. The republic's two inland waterways, the Syrdarya in south-central Kazakhstan and the Irtysh River in the northeast, have a total of 4,000 kilometers of waterway navigable by commercial craft. A state agency, the Kazakhstan River Fleet Industrial Association (Kazrechmorflot), administers river traffic. The development of a transport network in Kazakhstan under the USSR was carried on primarily to exploit the rich natural resources of the Republic and the transportation of these resources to the main industrial centers of the Soviet Union, as well as to provide links from the Central Asia Republics and Kazakhstan to the Central and Eastern parts of Russia.

The water transport system comprises 6 river ports and 2 seaports and is represented by many enterprises operating in the transport of freight and passengers, as well as cargo handling facilities in river ports and seaports. The inland waterways include: the rivers of Irtysh, Ural, Ili, Ishim, and Syrdarya; the water reservoirs of Bukhtarminskoye, Ust-Kamenogorskoye and Shulbinskoye; and the Balkhash and Zaisan Lakes.

The major seaports of the Caspian Sea are the Aktau commercial seaport and the Atyrau commercial seaport. Sea transport has limited possibilities for development owing to the isolated location of the Caspian Sea. The development of sea transportation of goods to Azerbaijan and the Islamic Republic of Iran depends on possible overloads of railway transport in this region.

Integration into the world trade system entails accelerated modernization of the Aktau seaport along with the development of regular marine hauling on the Caspian Sea. Reconstruction of the port, including the reconstruction of a breakwater and an underwater dam, the purchasing of equipment and the modernization of cranes will be completed using a loan from the European Bank for Reconstruction and Development. Eighty-eight percent of the cargo transported by river is composed of mineral and construction materials. In 2000, there was a 3.8-fold increase in the total volume of goods transported by water. However, since 2005 cargo transport by water has declined gradually; this is compensated by the gradual increases in passenger transport by water. The Irtysh is the main navigable river in the country, accounting for about 80 percent of cargo transported by river. The growing importance of the Caspian Sea as an international transport artery, the geographical location of Kazakhstan ports, and the potential of the country's oil and gas sector all provide potential for the fast development of sea transport in Kazakhstan. The Aktau commercial seaport is located on the eastern border of the Caspian Sea and is the only seaport carrying out international shipment of dry cargo, crude oil, and oil products. Today it provides connections with Iran, Transcaucasia and, via the rivers and canals of Russia, with the Black and Baltic seas.

Pipeline Transportation

The oil pipeline system was designed to ship domestic oil, most of which is extracted in the western part of the country, and to bring Russia's Siberian oil to refineries in Kazakhstan. In late March 2001, Kazakhstan opened the CPC (Caspian Pipeline Consortium) "Tengiz–Novorossiysk" pipeline. In May 1999, construction began of the 1,580 kilometer pipeline, dedicated to carrying Kazakhstan oil from the huge reserves of the Tengiz oil field (the sixth largest oil field in the world, with estimated recoverable reserves of 6 to 9 billion barrels) in western Kazakhstan to the Russian Black Sea port of Novorossiysk, which will serve as a link for transportation of Kazakhstan oil to the world markets. After putting the pipeline into full operation, about 28 million tons of oil will be transported annually. By 2030, the carrying capacity of the pipeline is expected to increase up to 67 million tons per year. The new pipeline will be the major export route for transportation of Tengiz oil to international markets, and it will potentially transform the country's oil and gas sector, as well as the economy. In 2005, 238.8 million tons of oil, petroleum products, and gas were transported through Kazakhstan's pipeline system. The total length of oil pipelines at the end of 2000 was 6,695.8 kilometers and gas pipelines – 10,137 kilometers. Freight transportation by pipeline accounted for more than one-quarter of total freight transported by all means in Kazakhstan.

TRANSPORTATION INDUSTRY STRATEGY

The mission of the transportation industry in Kazakhstan is to develop and maintain a transportation system that supports the economic growth of Kazakhstan. The transport complex of Kazakhstan is facing a series of basic strategic challenges in order to become more efficient. These include: Creation of a rational sovereign transport web integrated into the world transport system and providing Kazakhstan with access to the seas; Modernizing of existing rail and highways, waterways, ports, airports, and aero-navigation complexes; Creation of its own factory and repair stations of all types of transport; Building of an industry relating to the provision of modern communication facilities; Improvement of the control system and the normative and legal basis for the transport and communication complex.

2030 Development Strategy of Kazakhstan with a Focus on Transportation

The long-term priority is to support the infrastructure for the transport industry. Transportation streams from the East to the West and vice-versa, historically run on the territory of this country, and today their intensity does not fail. The task for Kazakhstan is in maintaining the competitiveness of a domestic transportation complex in the world market and increasing trade streams through her territory. Industry to a certain degree is developed enough, and should follow the long-term prospect strategy of concentrated growth consisting in diversification of national markets and in searching new markets, that are capable of taking advantage of its transportation services. This strategy will promote an increasing development of the motor industry, tourism, the service industry, roads, etc.

RECOMMENDATIONS

Because of the favorable geographic location of Kazakhstan, as well as the historical "Great Silk Road," the country continues to ensure transport corridors from the North to the South and from west to the east. The port of Aktau is a main part of the transport corridor for Europe-Asia transiting through the Caspian and Black seas, the Volga, the Volgo-Don and the Belomoro-Baltic canal, and also in the direction of Iran. The development of the container terminal in port Aktau opens up enormous opportunities for new traffic flows from Europe by transit through Azerbaijan and Georgia, from Arab countries by transiting through Iran, and also loads transported from China and Southeast Asia by transiting through Kazakhstan and to the countries of Europe.

In the long-term, the market of sea transportation will explicate in the following directions: the Iranian direction – forward water communication with export-import loads and transit in the Persian countries; the Russian direction – forward water communication with ports of the Russian Federation, Caspian (Makhachkala, Astrakhan) and Azov basins with export-import loads to the Russian Federation. It is necessary to mark a development program of the Russian ports in the Kaspiysky-Azov basin; Northern direction (forward water communication by means of the canal Volgo-Baltiy with export-import loads in the countries of the Baltic basin). The Iranian direction is characterized already by existing developed international trade with the countries of CIS, and the self-relative development of the port's existing ferry line Aktau-Baku-Noushakhr.

International and multimodal transport presents a special challenge for Kazakhstan because of its economic structure and unusual geographical characteristics. Indeed, although its main trading partners (Russia and Uzbekistan) are adjacent to Kazakhstan, traded goods must still traverse long distances over land and, to reach some key trading partners, must cross several transit countries. Ultimately, the cost of international transport is inevitably high and problems with the quality of transport (especially its speed and reliability, and the probability of damages) limit the benefits to be gained from trade. Kazakhstan herself is also an important transit country, which creates both opportunities and constraints.

Figure 4-8
Imports into Kazakhstan in 2005[20]

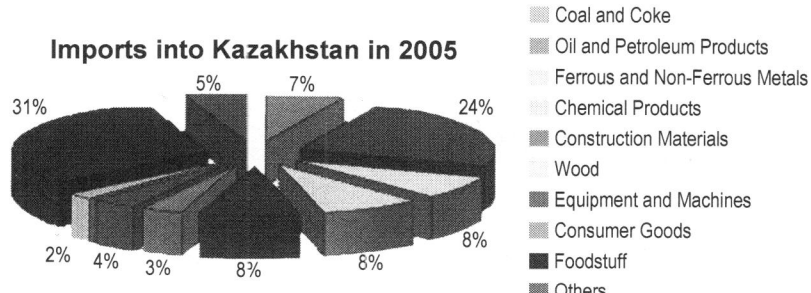

Coal and Coke, 7%; Oil and Petroleum Products, 24%; Ferrous and Non-Ferrous Metals, 8%; Chemical Products, 8%; Construction Materials, 8%; Wood, 3%; Equipment and Machines; 4%; Consumer Goods, 2%; Foodstuff, 31%; Others, 5%.

Figure 4-9
Exports from Kazakhstan in 2005

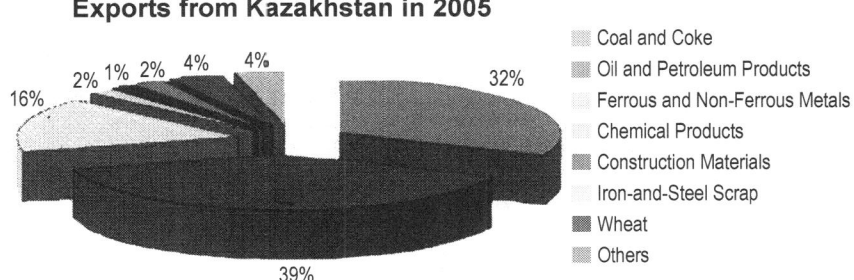

Coal and Coke, 32%; Oil and Petroleum Products, 39%; Ferrous and Non-Ferrous Metals, 16%; Chemical Products, 2%; Construction Materials, 1%; Wood, 3%; Iron-and-Steel Scrap; 2%; Wheat, 4%; Others, 4%.

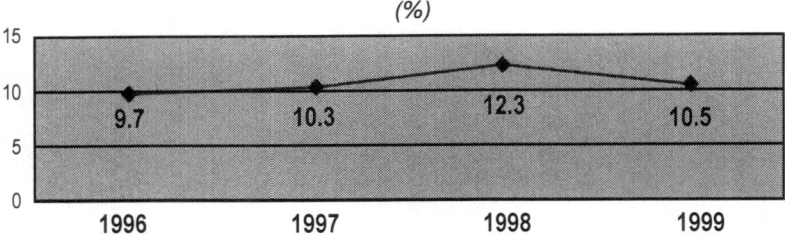

Figure 4-10
Contribution of Transportation Sector to GDP
(%)

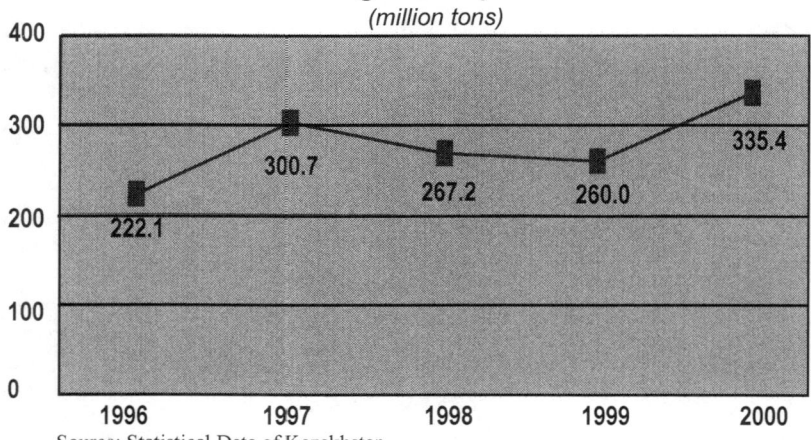

Figure 4-11
Freight Transported
(million tons)

Source: Statistical Data of Kazakhstan

Figure 4-12
Industry Breakdown of Kazakhstani Imports in 2001

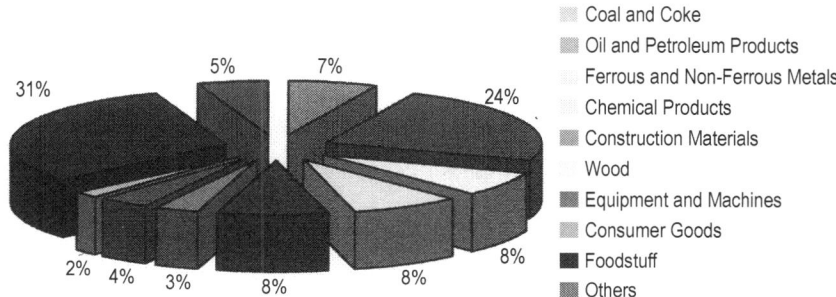

- Coal and Coke
- Oil and Petroleum Products
- Ferrous and Non-Ferrous Metals
- Chemical Products
- Construction Materials
- Wood
- Equipment and Machines
- Consumer Goods
- Foodstuff
- Others

Coal and Coke, 7%; Oil and Petroleum Products, 24%; Ferrous and Non-Ferrous Metals, 8%; Chemical Products, 8%; Construction Materials, 8%; Wood, 3%; Equipment and Machines; 4%; Consumer Goods, 2%; Foodstuff, 31%; Others, 5%.

Source: International Trade in Kazakhstan, Fourth International Conference "TransEurozlya-2002," Astana, 2002.

Figure 4-13
Industry Breakdown of Kazakhstani Exports in 2001
(Percent of Total Exports)

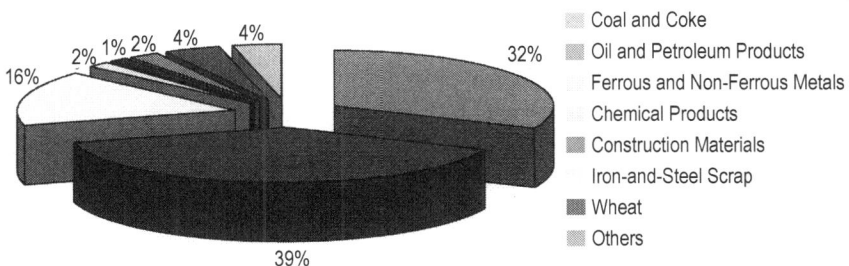

- Coal and Coke
- Oil and Petroleum Products
- Ferrous and Non-Ferrous Metals
- Chemical Products
- Construction Materials
- Iron-and-Steel Scrap
- Wheat
- Others

Coal and Coke, 32%; Oil and Petroleum Products, 39%; Ferrous and Non-Ferrous Metals, 16%; Chemical Products, 2%; Construction Materials, 1%; Iron-and-Steel Scrap, 2%; Wheat, 4%; Others, 4%.

Source: National Statistics Agency of Kazakhstan

Table 4-14
Various Modes of Transportation of Cargo
(mln.ton)

	1991	1992	1993	1994	1995	1996	1997	1998	1999	2000
Railways	328,194	289,398	220,524	175,44	161,1	140,15	136,456	129,953	123,935	156,396
Airlines	76	71	83	109	107	100	96	117	118	84
Auto	561.8	451	296.4	128.2	59.9	39.6	28.9	20	19.9	24.3
River	104	62	58	61	81	61	81	45	41	25
Pipe-lines	20.4	19.4	42.3	31.7	37.9	41.1	79.9	76.7	106.2	138.8

Source: Statistical Data of Kazakhstan

Figure 4-15
Public Transportation of Cargo
(mln. ton)

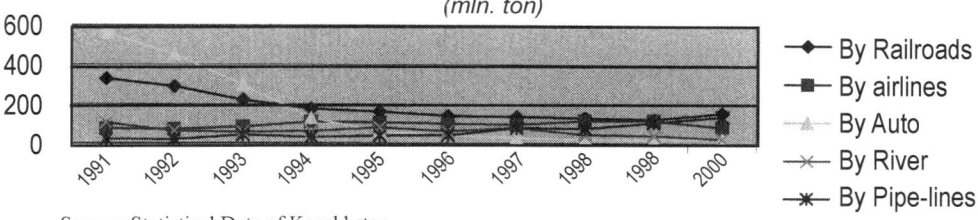

Source: Statistical Data of Kazakhstan

Table 4-16
Distribution of Transport Types
in Overall Passenger Usage
(%)

	1990	1995	2000
Taxi Motor	1	1	1
Urban	3	4	4
Airlines	19	15	10
Bus	49	40	28
Railways	28	40	57

Source: National Statistics Agency of Kazakhstan

Figure 4-17
Imports by Rail in 2001

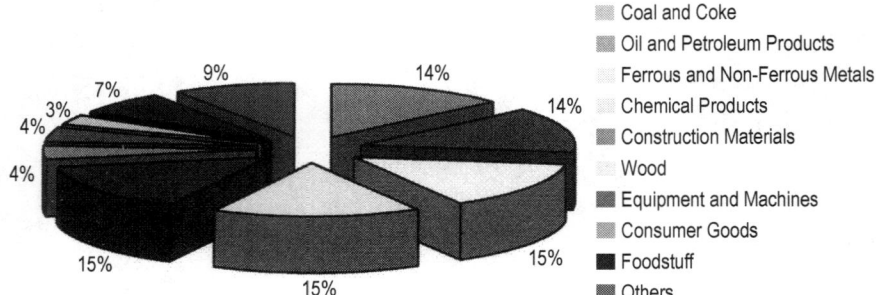

Coal and Coke, 14%; Oil and Petroleum Products, 14%; Ferrous and Non-Ferrous Metals, 15%; Chemical Products, 15%; Construction Materials, 15%; Wood, 4%; Equipment and Machines, 4%; Consumer Goods, 3%; Foodstuff, 7%; Others, 9%.

Source: National Statistics Agency of Kazakhstan

Figure 4-18
Exports by Rail in 2001

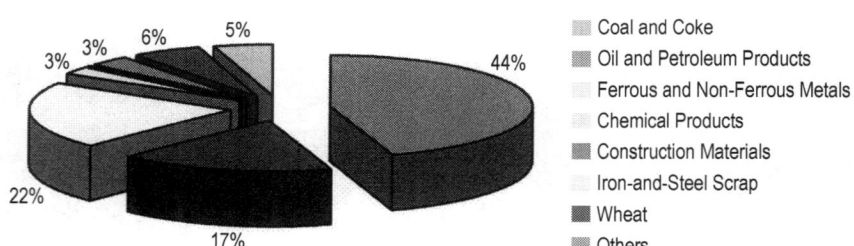

Coal and Coke, 44%; Oil and Petroleum Products, 17%; Ferrous and Non-Ferrous Metals, 22%; Chemical Products, 3%; Construction Materials, 0%; Iron-and-Steel Scrap; 3%; Wheat, 6%; Others, 5%.

Source: National Statistics Agency of Kazakhstan

Table 4-19
Transportation of Cargo by Public Railways, *mln tons*

	1996	1997	1998	1999	2000
Coal	71,440	69,148	68,442	58,258	74,128
Coke	65	196	86	61	249
Oil and oil products	12,688	13,593	14,309	15,295	17,747
Ore	15,438	19,159	11,320	23,009	29,361
Black metal	3,089	3,864	3,379	4,125	4,735
Crowbar of black metal	686	705	n/a	1,586	2,618
Chemical and mineral fertilizations	3,199	2,123	993	1,301	810
Mineral building cargos	n/a	6,318	7,042	5,577	7,580
Cement	978	501	473	680	967
Wood cargos	185	205	323	401	707
Bread cargos	4,413	5,116	517	4,805	7,339
Other cargos	27,969	15,528	19,069	8,837	10,155
Total	140,150	136,456	129,953	123,935	156,396

Source: National Statistics Agency of Kazakhstan

Table 4-20
Cargo Transportation by Public Railways *(%)*

	1996	1997	1998	1999	2000
Coal	51	50.7	52.7	47	47.4
Coke	0.05	0.1	0.07	0.05	0.16
Oil and oil products	9.1	9.9	11	12.3	11.3
Ore	11	14	8.7	18.6	18.8
Black metal	2.7	3.3	2.6	4.6	2.0
Chemical and mineral fertilizations	2.3	1.6	0.8	1.1	0.5
Mineral building		4.6	5.4	4.5	4.9
Cement	0.7	0.4	0.4	0.6	0.6
Wood	0.1	0.2	0.2	0.3	0.5
Bread	3.1	3.7	3.5	3.9	4.7
Other	20	11.4	14.7	7.1	6.5
Total	100	100	100	100	100

Source: National Statistics Agency of Kazakhstan

Figure 4-21
Imports via Highway in 2001

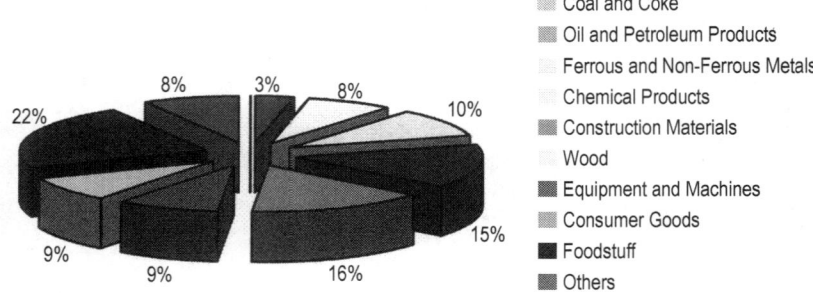

Coal and Coke, 0%; Oil and Petroleum Products, 3%; Ferrous and Non-Ferrous Metals, 8%; Chemical Products, 10%; Construction Materials, 15%; Wood, 16%; Equipment and Machines, 9%; Consumer Goods, 9%; Foodstuff, 22%; Others, 8%.

Source: National Statistics Agency of Kazakhstan

Figure 4-22
Exports via Highway in 2001

Coal and coke	0%
Oil and petroleum products	1%
Ferrous and non-ferrous metals	2%
Chemical products	3%
Construction materials	60%
Iron and Steel Scrap	3%
Wheat	13%
Others	18%

Source: National Statistics Agency of Kazakhstan

Figure 4-23
Trucks and Buses in Public Transportation
(number of units)

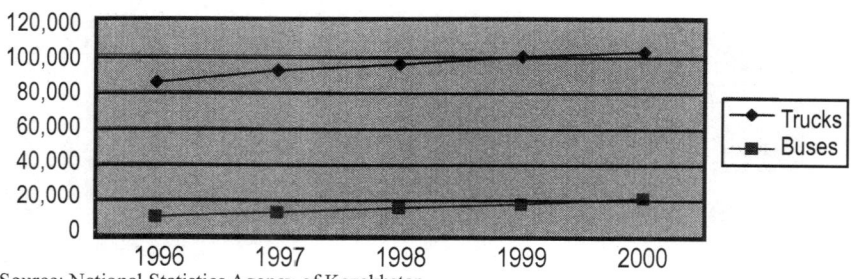

Source: National Statistics Agency of Kazakhstan

Figure 4-24
Airline Travel by Province
(mln passenger-km)

	1996	1997	1998	1999	2000
Akhmolinskaya	n/a	n/a	n/a	15.04	13.60
Akhtubinskaya	26.00	6.00	7.10	18.84	n/a
Almatinskaya	10.40	13.00	3.30	2.40	9.70
Atyrauskaya	53.90	59.00	56.00	47.50	85.70
Zhambylskaya	73.20	16.00	13.30	3.10	1.90
Karagandinskaya	293.30	392.00	21.90	16.13	17.00
Kostanaiskaya	105.70	n/a	n/a	n/a	n/a
Kysilardinskaya	14.80	18.00	6.40	3.50	n/a
Mangistauskaya	14.60	6.00	0.90	n/a	n/a
Pavlodarskaya	175.90	123.00	143.70	52.30	55.40
Astana (Capital city)	168.30	214.00	298.70	233.90	96.70
Almaty (Commercial center)	1961.80	340.00	243.90	328.94	152.30

Source: National Statistics Agency of Kazakhstan

Figure 4-25
Percent of Air Travel Passengers
(by Province)

	1996	1997	1998	1999	2000
Akhmolinskaya	n/a	n/a	n/a	n/a	8.1
Akhtubinskaya	13.3	5.4	3.0	20.5	8.1
Almatinskaya	10.0	10.0	18.2	6.4	15.9
Atyrauskaya	7.8	6.8	18.5	10.1	7.1
Zhambylskaya	6.5	5.8	9.5	2.3	9.5
Karagandinskaya	7.3	9.1	1.4	14.4	8.5
Kostanaiskaya	8.3	10.2	n/a	n/a	n/a
Kysilardinskaya	3.1	7.0	9.6	3.7	n/a
Mangistauskaya	7.1	8.2	2.0	n/a	n/a
Pavlodarskaya	8.0	8.0	16.7	5.4	9.5
Astana	9.7	8.0	13.7	7.7	5.0
Almaty	7.0	10.2	7.0	6.8	8.9

Source: National Statistics Agency of Kazakhstan

Figure 4-26
Airline Cargo Turnover
(in tons)

	1996	1997	1998	1999	2000
Akhmolinskaya	n/a	n/a	n/a	1,365.0	1,295.3
Akhtubinskaya	34.5	95.1	8.9	10.7	
Almatinskaya	250.1	59.9	53.7	19.4	1,891.0
Atyrauskaya	375.6	211.7	114.0	40.2	190.5
East-Kazakhstan	823.8	2,030.5	56.5	3,745.8	331.7
Zhambylskaya	756.5	1,498.6	1,463.4	4,178.5	0.9
West-Kazakhstan	n/a	n/a	n/a	n/a	n/a
Karagandinskaya	893.2	3,501.4	987.6	n/a	n/a
Kostanaiskaya	323.9	n/a	n/a	n/a	n/a
Kysilardinskaya	35.8	42.2	6.0	14.1	n/a
Mangistauskaya	59.4	35.6	4.4	n/a	n/a
Pavlodarskaya	529.9	378.4	638.5	153.9	183.2
North-Kazakhstan	368.7	28.8	6.9	n/a	n/a
South-Kazakhstan	23,605.9	10.1	n/a	492.7	16.3
Astana	1,732.8	922.0	2,891.1	2,179.7	3,159.0
Almaty	106,675.5	49,113.1	27,634.4	38,465.0	90,910.3

Source: National Statistics Agency of Kazakhstan

Figure 4-27
Transporting Cargo by Water
(mln. ton)

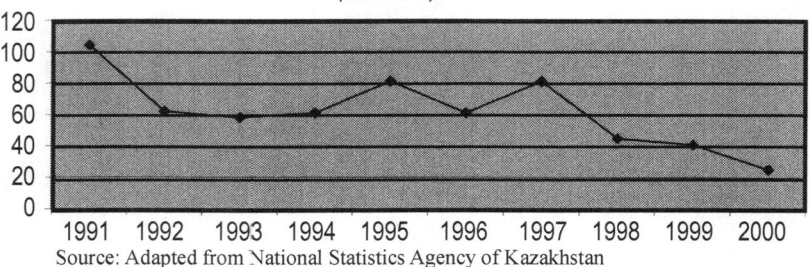

Source: Adapted from National Statistics Agency of Kazakhstan

Figure 4-28
Water Transport of Passengers
(million passenger-km)

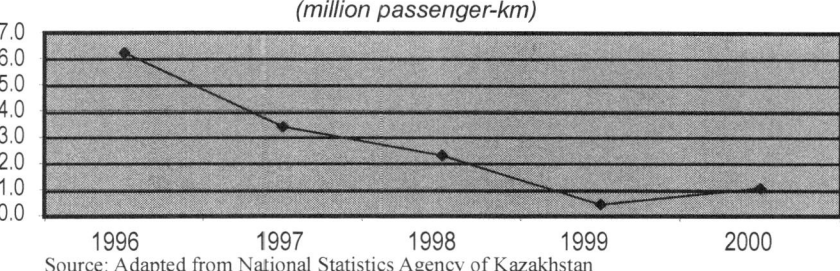

Source: Adapted from National Statistics Agency of Kazakhstan

Figure 4-29
Passengers Traveling via Water Transport
as Percent of All Passengers Using Public Transport
(%)

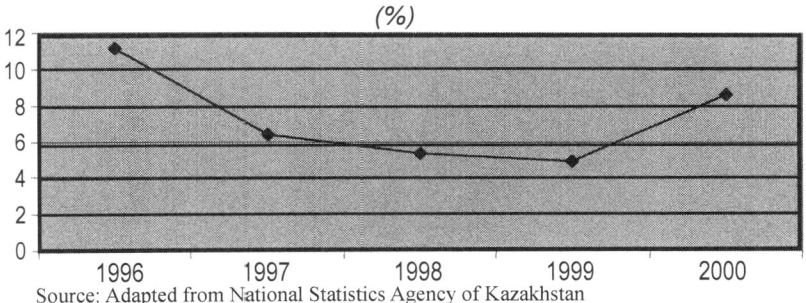

Source: Adapted from National Statistics Agency of Kazakhstan

Figure 4-30
Transportation of Freight through Pipelines
(million tons)

	1998	1999	2000
Total freight:	76.7	106.2	138.8
Gas	56.4	86.9	109.6
Oil	20.3	19.3	29.2

Source: Adapted from National Statistics
Agency of Kazakhstan

Figure 4-31
Freight Turnover via Pipelines
(billion tons-km)

	1998	1999	2000
Total freight:	27	34.7	50.9
Gas	11.6	17.9	30.6
Oil	15.4	16.8	20.3

Source: Adapted from National Statistics
Agency of Kazakhstan

Figure 4-32
Modal Economic Characteristics

Modal Economic Characteristics	Road	Rail	Air	Water
Cost	Moderate	Low	High	Low
Market Coverage	Door-to-Door	Terminal-to-Terminal	Terminal-to-Terminal	Same
Degree of Competition	Many	Moderate	Moderate	Few
Predominant Traffic	All Types	Low-Moderate Value, Moderate-High Density	High Value, Low-Moderate Density	Low Value, High Density
Average Length of Haul	Short to Long	Medium to Long	Medium to Long	Medium to Long
Equipment Capacity (tons)	10-25	50-12,000	5-125	3,000-15,000

Figure 4-33
Export/Import Company Shares

Item	Company	Market Share for export / import*, %
1	Tran system	25
2	KIF-Actobe	13
3	KIF-Almaty	5
4	Tranco	7
5	Akzar Trans	Not Available
6	Iscomtransservice	5
7	Kaztransservice	10

*Internal transportation excluded because they are not meaningful for comparison of freight forwarding companies.

Source: Transport in the Republic of Kazakhstan, *Statistical Data*

Chapter 5

The Retail Industry:
Recent Development in Kazakhstan

Introduction

Historically, until the time when the Soviet Union took over nearly 100 years ago, the people of the Central Asian steppe were nomadic and conducted their business in the traditional ways. That is, it was common to see caravan-style trading like the Great Silk Road until then, but that ended under Soviet control. Once the Soviet Union imposed its system, they were forced to abandon their ways: how then would they return to living in a free economy after generations under the Soviet system? The actions taken by President Nazarbaev, such as dismantling all of Kazakhstan's nuclear weapons, spoke clearly to the world of that nation's readiness to join the global economy. The people also understood the change. However, unlike the case of China, where Communist control lasted only a half century, Kazakhstan has seen five generations of Soviet dominance. So how can they make up for the natural development of the century they were deprived, and how can they get ready to join the global economy?

While it was not easy for the citizens of Kazakhstan to re-learn even the way of the past, it was natural for the retailing sector to re-start from the bottom-up out of necessity; i.e., exchange and/or buying/selling are the most fundamental activities in all societies, except among foragers, for survival. Whether it is street vending, door-to-door selling, buying and selling at a market place, or store front, people must get money to buy food and other necessities. In Kazakhstan also, when a person has no job or loses a job, he/she would turn to sell whatever he/she can as a source of income. Some would travel to other parts of the former Soviet Union as well as China or the Arab Emirates to buy goods, with the idea of selling them in Kazakhstan. In the period right after the independence, those goods could be sold with a mark-up of 100%, but it is reported that the standard mark-ups are now down to 15 to 20% due to increased competition among those traders. Consequently, this type of retailing activity seems to be waning, undoubtedly to be replaced by something more profitable.

However, the development of more dynamic and systematic distribution channels, etc., which is a natural part of the retailing business elsewhere, would take more time. For Kazakhstan, due to a lack of manufacturing activities under Soviet rule, the development of such distribution systems, from the manufacturers, to wholesalers, to retailers, and to consumers, as practiced in the free world, did not occur. As a consequence, they were also deprived of acquiring the standard business know-how of the rest of the world—let alone adapting to the global economy and its business practices. They had to acquire such knowledge in the period since her independence. So, while some may have anticipated that the Republic of Kazakhstan might or would develop a variety of business activities quickly because of her rich natural resources, the process of catching up has been rather slow. It is true particularly for her development of manufacturing and distribution systems, as mentioned before. The fact is that only a few ventures have reached the necessary volume of manufacturing to be profitable today, let alone reach the profit level that would encourage the further development of production facilities. As a result, combined with the fact that foreign business firms were quick and enthusiastic about selling their products there as soon as Kazakhstan became independent, retail is the fastest growing and the most developed business sector in Kazakhstan today.

As one can see from Figure 5-1, such influence exists even for the

Figure 5-1
Influences on Retailing

U.S. 1890-1950s	U.S. 1955-1970	U.S. 1990s
R.K. 1991-1995	R.K. 1995-1997	R.K. 1997-present
Small Retailers	Department Stores	Department Stores
Department Stores	Discount Stores	Discount Stores
		Factory Outlet Malls
		Large Discount Outlets

development of retailing businesses. Most retailing activities take place inside stores or service establishments, but may also be conducted outside the usual store settings, such as through telemarketing, vending machines that were developed in Kazakhstan, and also mail order catalog. In Kazakhstan today, there exist all the basic types of retail business, such as department stores, supermarkets, specialty stores, discount stores, and cash and carry, as in other countries, though still rather limited.

Among all retailing business, one might note that the retailing of electronic goods is the most competitive in Kazakhstan today. The leading local retailing networks are Planet of Electronics, Technopole, Levita, Sulpak, Glotur, ALSI, Ardo and Trade Houses—Sukj Watm Ak-Pharabi, Zangar and Adem, which are Kazakhstani companies as shown in Figure

Figure 5-2
Market Shares of Electronic Goods Retailers in 2002
(%)

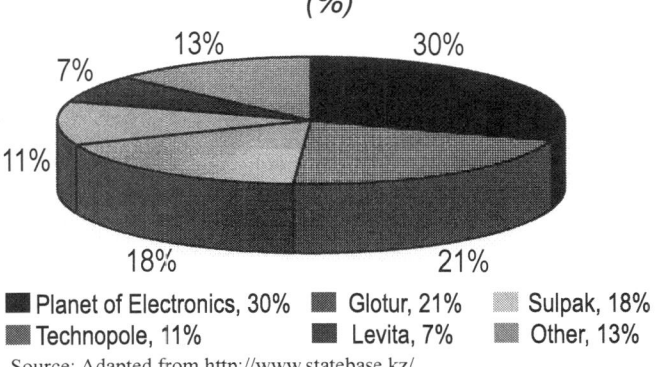

■ Planet of Electronics, 30%   ■ Glotur, 21%   ▨ Sulpak, 18%
▨ Technopole, 11%   ■ Levita, 7%   ▨ Other, 13%

Source: Adapted from http://www.statebase.kz/

5-2. There are foreigners and foreign-owned retail businesses that have local partners with 51% of equity ownership. However, there are legal restrictions on permanent land-use (i.e., the outright purchase of land) by foreigners; leasing or renting buildings as retail business centers are permitted.

While the retailing business of electric/electronic goods accounts for only about 20% of the total retail spending, and less than a quarter of a percent of the total retailing transactions in Kazakhstan, this is the sector of the retailing business that is probably the most adaptive to the global economy, and hence, leading the nation's retailing business of the future. Therefore, we will be discussing that here.

The objectives of the retailers are not unique to Kazakhstan. As for retailers everywhere, the retail industry of electric/electronic goods emphasizes the importance of (1) increasing market share not only in such economic and urban centers as Almaty and Astana but in other cities as well; (2) increasing product range; (3) increasing the brand awareness of the retailing network; and (4) improving customer service and after-sale services. Retailing networks must adjust to the internal and external environment of the industry, which is highly competitive, and involves non-price competition as well as price competition. The retailers also acknowledge the importance of offering a full range of services and adding value to customers as their strategy. At present, all the world's well-known brands and products are sold in Kazakhstan, and different products and brands are targeted at different market segments, depending on the target users—namely low, middle, or high-end households and also commercial customers. Thus, while the whole industry's goal is for growth, each retailer has its own strategy to suit different types of customers.

As to the industry governance, the Ministry of Industry and Trade regulates the retail industry. The structure of the ministry consists of the Departments of (1) Economic Policy, (2) Investment Policy, (3) Foreign Economy, (4) Industrial Policy, (5) Regional Policy, and (6) Committees.

The major functions of the Ministry are stated as: (a) development of plans for foreign trade and the international affairs of Kazakhstan; (b) development and realization of the national foreign trade policy; and (c) coordination of the relationship between industries and business with foreign economic affairs. The Ministry defines priorities regarding foreign trade policy; develops appropriate plans in terms of external economic relations; establishes the standard for foreign trade in collaboration with other ministries; coordinates activities with regard to the policies of Kazakhstan's WTO (World Trade Organization) membership; develops the standard for customs regulation; prepares proposals for improving the national trade balance; proposes recommendations for improving and updating foreign trade policies and economic relationships with other nations; and analyzes the current situation and trends in the global economy. Various departments are in charge of (1) preparing economic strategy; policy and forecasts of industry's development, including manufacturing, retailing, construction, transportation, telecommunication, agriculture, science, and tourism; developing antimonopoly activities; and planning the socio-economic development of major industries; (2) coordinating the areas of the economic development of geology, geography, mapping, the energy sector, non-ferrous and black metals, chemical oil and gas, coal, transport, telecommunication, and the retailing and agricultural sectors; and (3) proposals for developing national economic policy for various industrial sectors.

Norms of the Retail Industry

As stated before, manufacturing activities in Kazakhstan are not yet well developed as of now, and the retail industry of electronic goods is distributing mostly foreign-made products, i.e., Korean, Japanese, and European manufacturers, such as Daewoo, Samsung, LG, Philips, and others. It is obvious, therefore, that multinational corporations are present, and the norms of the industry are influenced by those foreign corporations that are partners with the dealers, distributors, retailers, and local operators. The local retailers adapt and conform to the different merchandising programs of such foreign business concerns, but they would also take into consideration the cultural values of Kazakhstan as well; customers do not pay attention to brands so long as the product is of acceptable quality. In this sense, at present, due to the lack of too many choices and buyer knowledge, customer values and behavior are more focused on the basic functionality of products. Figure 5-3 shows the retailing structure since

Figure 5-3

Retailing Structure Since Independence
(Central Europe, Japan, US)

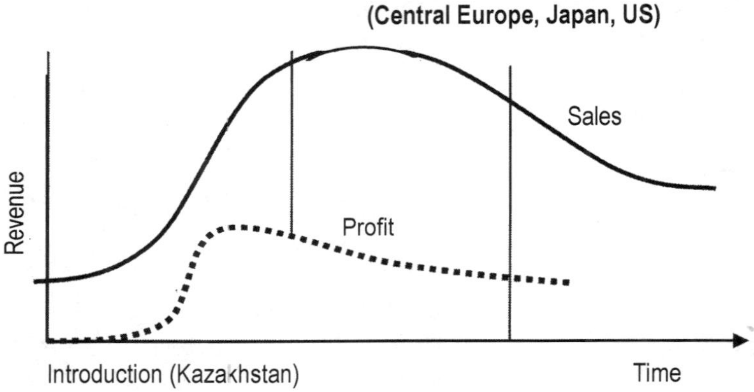

independence.

Additionally, it is interesting to see some new industrial norms emerging as well. These new businesses are now run by young ambitious people who are risk takers. Their beliefs, expectations, and value systems differ considerably from those during the Soviet period. Technological changes made the past approach to retailing antiquated and thus created conditions for healthy competition. Globalization of business made all global trade processes necessary for any national market. And the recent development of improving the credit system has allowed more players to enter the retail industry lately.

During the long period under the Soviet Union, the retail industry suffered, with government-owned stores and consumer co-operatives, as shown in Figure 5-4. Now, the Republic of Kazakhstan and the retail industry enjoy the benefits of globalization and internationalization as an unavoidable modern trend. It can be stated that the companies in the retail industry today are flexible and accepting of the changing conditions of the new environment. That is, the norms of the industry suit the objectives and strategies of the companies and representatives operating in it. In addition, such social and cultural changes are opening up new opportunities as shown in Figure 5-5 for the retailers and the industry as a whole.

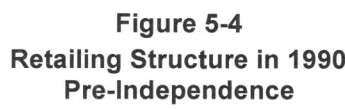

Figure 5-4
Retailing Structure in 1990
Pre-Independence

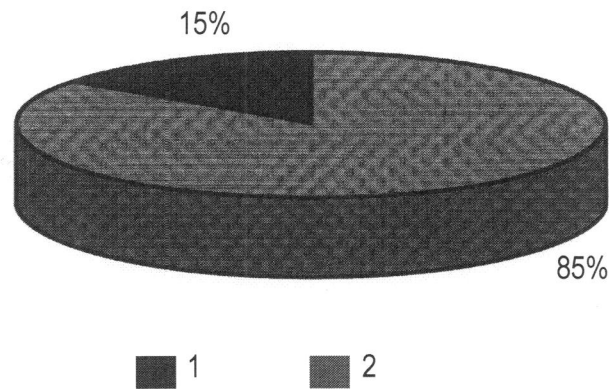

15%

85%

1   2

1. Government-owned stores and shops (85%)
2. Consumer co-operatives (15%)
Source: www.statebase.kz

Currently, Kazakhstan is home to chain stores such as Planet of Electronics and Ardager. However, they, as most retail outlets, have many problems, such as poor quality of in-store management, unqualified personnel, inventory mishandling, and unclear positioning. But they are making some improvement gradually, especially in terms of service level and physical structure. There is a growing tendency to present a wider range of products and brands based on market research studies, and offer the brands that are in high demand. As to the price range, the retailers seem to focus on all segments of customers' economic and social status, high, middle, and low-income, hoping to keep all customers by offering something they like. As most retailers are still unable to compare with the service level and the price (the cost of goods sold) of the product with others, it becomes a major competitive advantage for customers. Bringing down the COGS (cost of goods sold) enables larger retailers to keep prices competitive. Larger retailers also have the advantage of accepting payment on credit sales through banks. In some cases, in-store promotional activities include certain brand name days, e.g., "LG day," and sweepstakes with purchase coupons. Public relations activities would be a participation in national contests like "Choice of the year," or "Brand of the year," a sponsorship of social campaigns, internet advertising, direct marketing, and offering monthly booklets. The physical structure of a "one-style-chain store" is becoming quite popular as that saves promotion costs due to customers' immediate recognition. Besides, uniformity and consistency are practiced among department stores. Improvement of service is being observed in many retail outlets. One would notice that the use of modern technology, such as checkout and in-store cameras, is spreading among

Figure 5-5
Retailing Structure in 2000

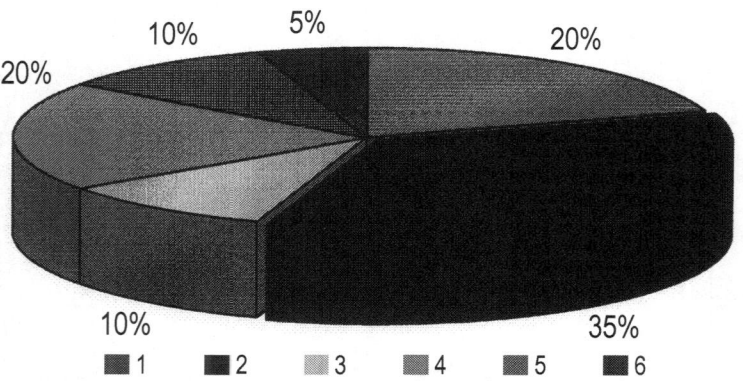

1. An unaffiliated or independent retailer who owns and operates only one retail outlet, 20%
2. A chain retailer or corporate retailer with multiple retail outlets, 35%
3. A franchise system, between a franchiser and a franchisee, 10%
4. A Leased Department (a retail store rented to a third party), 20%
5. Vertical Market System, 10%
6. Consumer Co-operative, 5%

Source: Adapted from http://www.statebase.kz/

retailers. To distinguish themselves many retailers stress the importance of having sales personnel with experience and good training. Also, in order to motivate employees, a bonus compensation system is introduced as well. As to location, retailers prefer a location with heavy traffic and also with good parking areas. The importance of supplier cooperation is being recognized and a means to enhance it is gradually implemented.

As with regard to retail finance anywhere, the financial strategy is critical for the retailers of electronic goods in order to ensure a sustained growth. It implies that the companies should sustain growth that could be achieved with no external equity financing, while maintaining a constant debt/equity ratio. Currently, however, the financial objective for the electronic goods retailing industry is to increase the operating profit margin through increased inventory turnover by increasing sales, and decreasing the not-value-adding costs. Despite the current difficult trading conditions, in terms of competition within the electronic retailing sector, the companies increase their profit through competitive pricing and overall total cost effectiveness as shown in Figure 5-6. This particular retail industry is characterized by seasonal sales: the highest sales are in June, July, and November, December. The high sales in June and July are due to the sales of air conditioners and refrigerators in the hot weather. But operating margins have been dropping as this industry is forced to

Figure 5-6
Logistics System

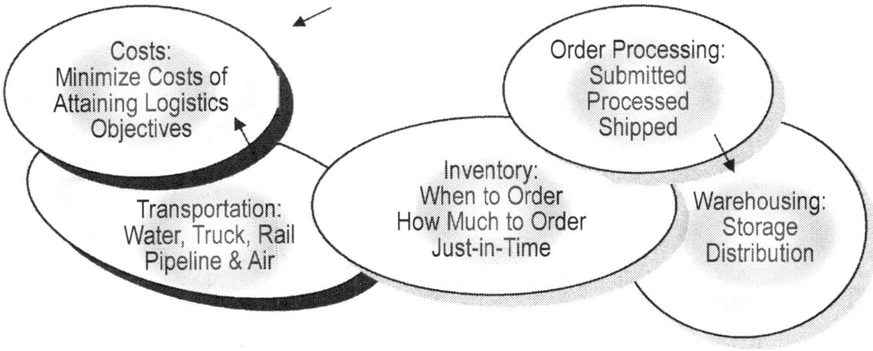

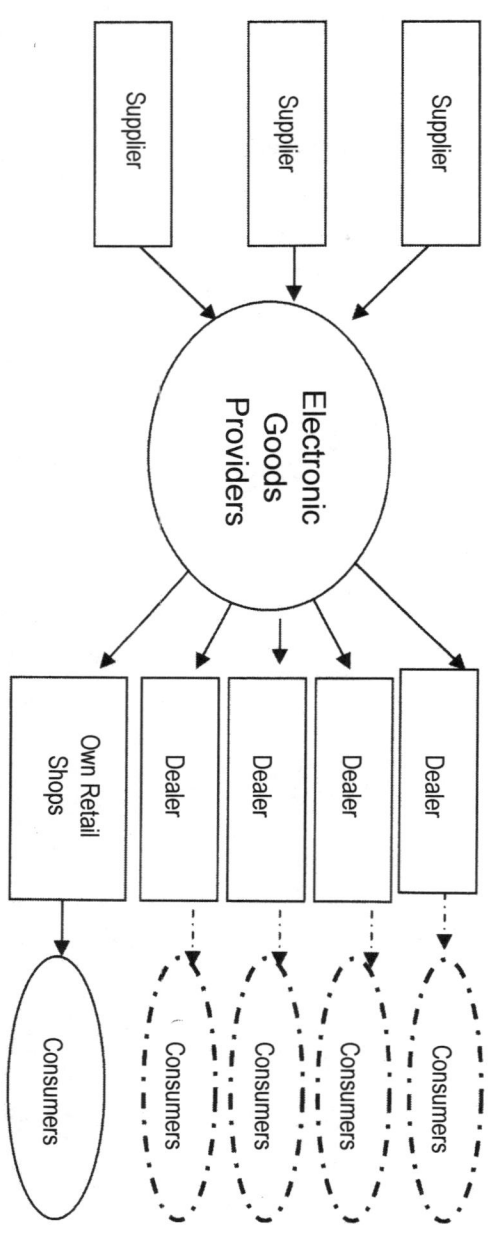

Figure 5-7
Supply Chain

keep prices low in order to meet high competition while the costs keep on increasing.

The key success factors for the retailing industry of electronic goods are as follows: (1) full-line of products; (2) high quality of products; (3) cost efficiency in non-value-added activities, i.e., transportation, inventory handling, general and administrative expenses; (4) high turnover of inventory; (5) aggressive marketing; (6) high brand awareness; (7) broad geographic coverage; (8) high quality of sales and after-sales services; and (9) good partnership with suppliers and distribution channels.

Supply Chain for Retailing Electric/Electronic Goods

Kazakhstan's logistics system, not very unique from other countries, consists of five elements, as discussed below, to support the function of logistics and reflect the overall strategies of the industry. That would provide customers with high quality goods quickly and in a timely fashion through an advanced logistics system that is characterized by (1) the ability to handle various products, (2) meeting the scheduled time, (3) the maximum number of geographic points being served all over Kazakhstan, and (4) minimum costs.

Those firms operate through an integrated supply chain, as shown in Figure 5-7, and make decisions to optimize logistics with the following considerations: (1) taking the data gathered by market demand analysis, and identifying new prospective customers as well as exploring new suppliers who might bring more profit while sustaining relations with the ongoing suppliers; (2) improving their contracts regarding prices, assortment, quality, and the time and mode of delivery; (3) keeping good records of the products that arrive in warehouses, such as date, category, brand name, description of model, and quantity, so that the records of the products received are kept accurately in the main office; (4) processing customer orders and entering them into the information system immediately, sending invoices, and then receiving payment from the customers. After that, the invoices go to the warehouses where the inventories are assigned to the orders. Then the orders are completed and delivered to the customers, and in this way the inventory records are able to be kept accurately. This process enables them to identify stock and reorder quantity levels in the warehouse.

One would find world-famous companies such as Sony, Panasonic, Thompson, Merton, LG, Samsung, Siemens, Philips, Grunding, and others in Kazakhstan for this business of selling electric and electronic products. As seen in Figure 5-8, and the merchandise is shipped to retailers by various means. White goods (refrigerators or washing machines), brown goods (TVs or telephones), DAP (domestic appliance products) and others under various brand names are delivered to their respective warehouses, either directly by the manufacturers or via transportation companies. These

Figure 5-8
Transportation Modes

Rail	Nation's largest carrier, cost-effective For shipping bulk products, piggyback	50%
Truck	Flexible in routing & time schedules, efficient For short-hauls of high value goods	46%
Water	Low cost for shipping bulky, low-value goods, slowest form	2%
Air	High cost, ideal when speed is needed or to ship High-volume, low-bulk items	2%

Source: http://www.marketing-tovar.kz/2002/06/02.htm

products are supplied from the countries of origin, which are all over the world, as the suppliers have signed contracts to ship them to Almaty by various modes of transportation whether it may be railroad, cargo boat as an intermediate chain, or trucks.

Interestingly, some dramatic changes in this industry are taking place as many manufacturers of these electric/electronic products are beginning to sell them not only through the existing chain of dealers but also by establishing subsidiaries of their own by building new plants. Therefore, the current mode of transportation will be more likely to change considerably and more trucking is expected in the future as shown in Figure 5-9.

These companies establish their distribution channels through a system of dealerships in different regions of Kazakhstan. This eliminates the need to have many distribution centers to serve different regions, and, instead, now they have large warehouses in two major cities, Almaty and Astana—locations with convenient railway access. In this way, they can

Figure 5-9
Performance of Transportation Modes

Criteria \ Alternatives	Railway	Highways	Air
Delivery speed	3	2	1
Delivery dependability	2	3	1
Loss and damage	3	2	1
Cost	1	2	3

1-best performance   3-worst performance
Source: http://www.projectshub.com/projects

handle larger quantities of goods, which is required for supplying a larger and wider range of products to meet the growing consumer demands while reducing transportation costs.

While suppliers in general prefer to use railways, and a major portion of the goods arrives in Kazakhstan by railway, some products such as DAP (domestic appliance product) come by trucks from Europe because of the transportation cost advantage in such cases. When the railroad is used for transportation, goods first arrive in containers by railway line before products reach the warehouses; then, after completing the customs procedures, the goods are unloaded by cranes and loaded on Lorries. Then the companies distribute their goods in Almaty by using their own Lorries, and the cost for this portion of delivery is sometimes absorbed by the companies, i.e., with no cost to customers. As for regional areas, the distribution of goods is made through a dealers' network without offering delivery service to customer homes. The transport modality and service capability are shown in Figure 5-9

Challenges for the Retail Infrastructure

As one might expect, there are many industry-wide problems that retailing companies face today. One major problem is the high rate of damage that occurs while white goods, e.g., refrigerators, etc., are being transported by railways. This is caused by the fact that the standard of railroad gauges in the CIS's (Commonwealth of Independent States) countries is not uniform; namely, the goods and vans from Europe have to be unloaded and re-loaded several times before the goods reach their final destinations. This makes it very difficult for the supplying companies to meet the customers' demands (as shown by the map of Kazakhstan in the Eurasian region) and poses a great challenge to any retailing chain to cover all the vast geographic area it must cover. Unfortunately for the retailing business in Kazakhstan, there is no cross-docking in any part of the country, since there are multiple container sizes and the number of distribution centers (DCs) in different regions of Kazakhstan poses a serious challenge to the retail industry. The retail industry's strengths and weaknesses are illustrated in Figure 5-10.

As far as the strength of the retailers handling electric/electronic products in Kazakhstan is concerned, first, most of them operate with a full-line of products because their customers prefer to buy them from the store that displays as wide a range of products as possible, rather than from the store with a limited line of products; e.g., only washing machines. Second, the retailers have already learned how to deal with rather sophisticated consumer tastes for the past ten-plus years. Moreover, almost all of them are in a strong financial position, notwithstanding the fact that they practice the policy of lower prices than those in other countries. At any rate, turnover of merchandise is their most serious concern and the key if they want to expand, or even to maintain, their business in the future.

One serious concern, however, is that, since electronic products are durable goods, when those goods saturate the market, they cannot expect to have the current level of need. In the near future, it will shift primarily to replacement purchases and service. So, the retailers will have to meet the new challenge. In addition to the current practice of aggressive promotion as the major marketing strategy in order to keep customers for a store with particular brands, they must shift the focus of research and development from attracting customers (e.g., with a good location and attractive exterior) to strengthening customer loyalty by improving customer service. As for their strong emphasis today on maintaining strong relationships with suppliers, when suppliers must compete with each other, the burden will naturally shift from the retailers to the suppliers to maintain good customer relations.

Perhaps the matter that poses a more serious challenge is the non-value-added cost. According to value chain analysis, the value-added activities are represented by marketing, sales, and after-sales services, amounting

Figure 5-10
Analysis of Strategic Factors
Strengths & Weaknesses

Strengths	Weaknesses
Stable financial position and strong cash flows	Damage and loss during transportation
Full-line of products	Lack of professional sales and office personnel
Low prices	Absence of integrated information technology (Extranet-Intranet)
About 10 years experience in retailing	Poorly developed motivation system for office staff
Aggressive promotion	Lack of experience in developing advertising campaign
Established relationship with suppliers	Geographic coverage
Conventional location and renovation of old shops	

to 3.3% of the cost of goods sold. The installation, repair, training, parts supply, and product adjustment are estimated to be 4.7% of the cost of goods sold. On the other hand, the non-value-added costs are the highest portion of the entire cost, which is 92% of the cost of goods sold. As mentioned earlier, the differentiation strategy could be achieved through investing in marketing and services, and decreasing the cost of outbound logistics. For that reason, it is important to break down this cost in a more detailed structure. The analysis could be done without dividing the products into brown and white categories, i.e., TVs and refrigerators, because the composition of the cost is practically the same for both categories. Of the outbound logistics costs, the suppliers' price is 67%, order processing costs 2%, transportation and tariffs are 17%, warehousing and inventory handling, 6%, and others account for 8%. One can see that the price they pay the suppliers is the highest portion of the outbound logistics cost, and the retailers hope to lower this by establishing a long-term relationship with suppliers. As to the cost for transportation, the problem of un-unified railroad gauges, in particular, cannot be helped unless the government would one day unify the railroad gauges throughout the geographic region. Other costs could be reduced by investing in new integrated information technologies, both external and internal.

Retailing of Other Sectors, e.g., Garment, and Other Consumer Goods

Due to the lack of manufacturing activities in Kazakhstan even as late as today, much of the consumer goods is imported from other countries, such as China, Turkey and others. For example, clothing for women made in China was heavily imported in the early stage of independence, but some serious problems developed so that it is now replaced with clothing from any other countries that can compete with price for the traders' business. Many clothing items made in Turkey are quite popular among office girls and professional women, for young working women are becoming rather fashion conscious as well.

In urban areas, there has been a considerable development of shopping centers or shopping zones with many stores clustering together, often several two-story buildings each housing a variety of stores within: toy shop, women's clothing store, book store, men's attire, and so on, and sometime with a coffee shop. This might very well be suited to the Kazakhstani shoppers' traditional preference to buy what they need in one location, as discussed earlier for the electronic/electric goods. Many large food stores, resembling American grocery stores, are also very conspicuously present in the urban centers, closely located to the above-mentioned multi-store buildings. The most retail business establishments are run by the Russians who did not leave Kazakhstan after the independence, or Russian-Kazakhstanis in some cases as of now. However, when the local population begins to manufacture a variety of products locally, we can anticipate that the structure of retailing business channels will become similar to that of the West, that is, to have well-developed chains with major manufacturers, wholesalers, and retail merchants. The current situation of the majority of people working and deriving their income from government jobs will, inevitably though slowly, change as local manufacturing activities develop.

Conclusion

Kazakhstan's retailers are like others anywhere, in that they all desire to make more profit by selling more, by making their store better known to the customers, having broad product ranges, and expanding into new regional markets. So, they aggressively promote themselves. Modern and attractive specialty stores with convenient locations are becoming common today in Kazakhstan. Also, retailers are targeting their specific segment of the market; i.e., high, middle, and low-income groups, or the general population. While they try to keep highly motivated employees and stress the importance of customer satisfaction, they also embrace supply-chain management as well. Currently, some supermarkets such as Uzhnyi and Ardager, and trade centers such as Ramstore, City Center, Adem, and Silkway, are emerging. Cities with high growth potential include Astana, Aktan, and Shymkent, and Pavlodar. According to the analysis by the Kazakhstan retail industry, a high level of investment in marketing is required, and also non-value-added costs must be reduced. Therefore, it is necessary to consider the integration of the supply chains of the retailing industry of electric/electronic goods as shown in Figure 5-11. One must note that the suppliers of new materials and manufacturers represent inbound logistics and the retailing business includes outbound logistics, marketing and service as indicated in Figure 5-12.

The retailers adapted the standard marketing strategies, such as maximizing availability of goods, channels, increasing the number of regional distributors, and also adapting the pricing policy by adjusting it to each region's purchasing power and demand. Some are also developing Internet marketing, e.g., a web site. A new trend is that people are following the Western-style shopping pattern of making all purchases in one store.

In the Western world, on-line retailing, or e-tailing, transactions account for about 20% of total retail spending; but it is less than 1% in Kazakhstan. In the U.S., the use of online, virtual stores is a complement to the location-specific stores. But the situation in Kazakhstan is so different and the future of online retailing is uncertain, at least for the near future, because of the limited penetration of computers and use of the Internet among the people.

The fact that McDonald's food cafes are not open in Kazakhstan, and there are not many people visiting Baskin & Robbins, can be explained by the largest segment of the population being older generation. They are very slow to get rid of the old ways under the Soviet Union, and that makes it difficult for them to accept the new Western forms of stores.

We can anticipate that the manufacturing sector of Kazakhstan will soon develop fully, whether it be articles of consumption such as garments, food processing, office supplies, etc., or durable goods. The retail industry of Kazakhstan will become very much like the rest of the world. Supported by the great wealth of natural resources with which the country is so fortunate to be endowed, Kazakhstan is expected to be a fine market for the producers of manufactured goods from the rest of the world. However, the most important matter, particularly for Kazakhstan's retailers, is that they all must shed the old Soviet mentality and replace that with the idea of meritocracy. It is imperative that they reject the old idea of relying solely on being clever at business as a means to achieve success, including the common practice today of cheating foreign visitors for a quick profit. In other words, they must instead embrace values such as a sense of integrity, fairness, hard work, appreciation for competence, and doing one's best for the common good. In this way the nation will regain the national pride of its long past, and younger generations will be able to do so. Then, Kazakhstan will be very successful, and she will be on a par with the rest of the post-industrial societies in the world. In the country where nearly 70% of the working population earns their income from working for the government, it is essential for the people to shift their basic psychology for business—otherwise, the retail sector will be completely taken over by the Russians and other foreign nationals.

102

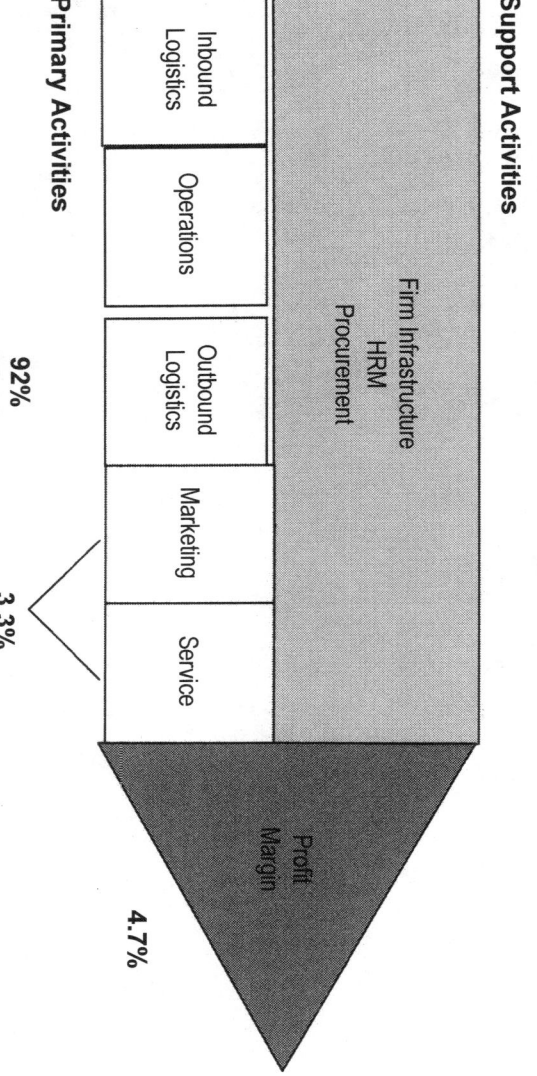

Figure 5-12

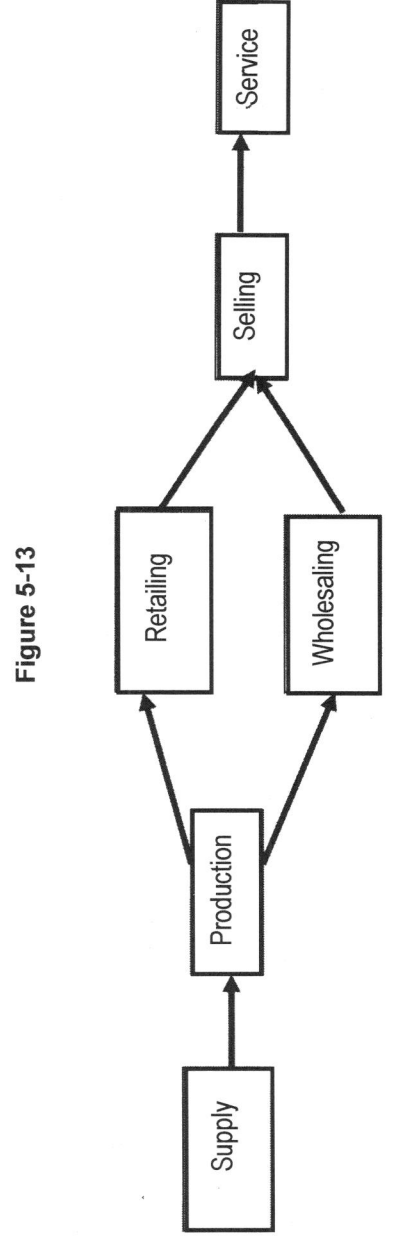

Figure 5-13

Figure 5-14
Percentage Change in Price for Nonfoods
(by regions)

REGIONS	2001	1999-2000
The Republic of Kazakhstan	4.5	6.1
Astana	5.9	5.5
Aktubinsk	3.3	6.3
Almaty	3.0	2.7
Atyrau	7.0	6.3
Eastern Kazakhstan	8.4	7.1
Djambul	1.1	3.6
Western Kazakhstan	3.5	3.6
Karaganda	4.2	5.1
Kostanai	1.5	3.4
Kyzyl Orda	7.3	11.2
Mangistau	6.7	4.3
Pavlodar	3.7	5.5
Northern Kazakhstan	3.0	6.3
Southern Kazakhstan	5.7	4.5
Astana City	3.4	8.8
Almaty City	4.2	10.2

Source: Agency of the Republic of Kazakhstan on Statistics,
Consumer market in 2001, pp. 5-7

Chapter 6

The Copper Industry:
A Quasi-Privatization at Work in the
Post-Soviet Republic of Kazakhstan

Introduction

Before independence, Kazakhstan's copper industry, like other sectors of the economy, was centrally planned and controlled by the Soviet Union. All natural resources (see Figure 6-15) including copper were under government control. After Kazakhstan became an independent republic, the present government allowed private investment (both domestic and foreign), yet kept a major share of ownership for itself.

Copper is not only the world's oldest metal used by man—dating back 10,000 years—but in today's global and modern economies, it has multifaceted uses, and its demand in a variety of consumer and industrial markets has grown exponentially. It is no wonder that, in the 21st century, the need for copper continues to grow; computers, telecommunications, automobiles, and other industries require copper. Demand for copper in the years 1988 and 2002 by country are presented as a pie chart (see Figure 6-3).

It is clear that the consumption of copper in China and other parts of Asia has changed dramatically, showing a substantial increase in demand. Copper is an important contributor to the national economies of mature, newly developed and developing countries; therefore the mining, processing, recycling, and transforming of the metal into a multitude of

Figure 6-1
Industries Using Copper

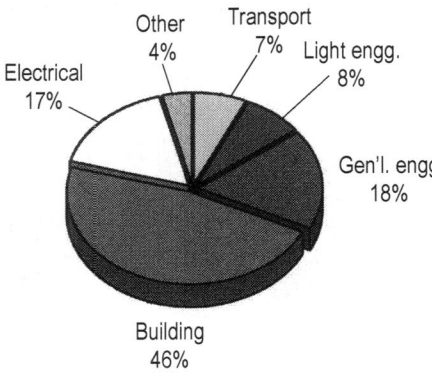

Source: www.mineral.ru

products create jobs and generate wealth. These activities contribute to building and maintaining a country's infrastructure, and create trade and investment opportunities. This is also particularly important for lesser-developed countries seeking to improve their living standards.

The countries with copper mines are: Chile, the U.S.A., Canada, Russia, Indonesia, Australia, Peru, Kazakhstan, China, Zambia, Poland, the Philippines, and Zaire. The largest mining companies in the world are Codelco and Minera Escondida of Chile (of which 57.5% is owned by BHP of Australia), and Phelps Dodge in the United States, followed by RTZ, Asarco, Freeport, ZCCM, Cyprus, and MIM. Kazakhstan is famous for its huge deposits of mineral wealth. Kazakhstan has significant reserves of copper (See the Minerals Map of Kazakhstan) and the country is among the world's largest copper producers and exporters.

In terms of material wealth, Kazakhstan ranks second among the CIS countries in reserves of copper, which is equal to 38% of all CIS reserves. The gross value of the explored and provisionally estimated material wealth in the subsoil of Kazakhstan amounts to over 2 trillion US dollars. Their mineable value is 1.1 trillion US dollars. The major industries where copper is used and their usage distribution are shown in Figure 6-1. The consumption of copper is increasing each year. This trend is illustrated in Figure 6-2.

The mineral output and raw material production of Kazakhstan greatly exceeds her domestic needs. It is worth noting that Kazakhstan exports 90% of refined copper. In 1999, the share of copper and copper products constituted almost 11% of the country's total exports; that figure increased to 19% in 2005, and has grown since then. This has created a positive investment climate during the past 5 years, and the major part of this investment was spent on the extraction of major mineral resources.

Eighty-one percent of these investments were from foreign countries. Huge amounts of investments have been directed to copper mining industries (See Figures 6-6 and 6-7) and it continues to grow. The main areas of investment are: development of the ore base, technology, equipment and upgrading of concentrating mills, as well as copper smelteries. A portion of investments is set aside for developing the infrastructure and the social sphere.

Figure 6-2
Statistics on the Worldwide Consumption of Copper

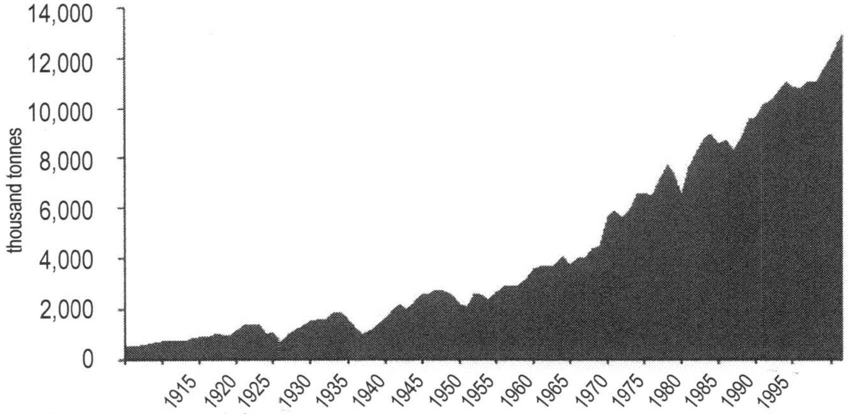

Source: www.copperinfo.com

The biggest corporation in the copper mining and processing industry is Kazakhmys, which is managed by Samsung Deutschland Corporation. Such corporations as Zhezkazgantsvetmet, Balkhashmys, VostochnoKazakhstanski MHK and Zheskentsky OK came together to form Kazakhmys. According to ranking by Copper Mine output Kazakhstan (Kazakhmys) took tenth position (See Figure 6-8) in world markets.

Figure 6-3
Copper Demand by Countries and Regions

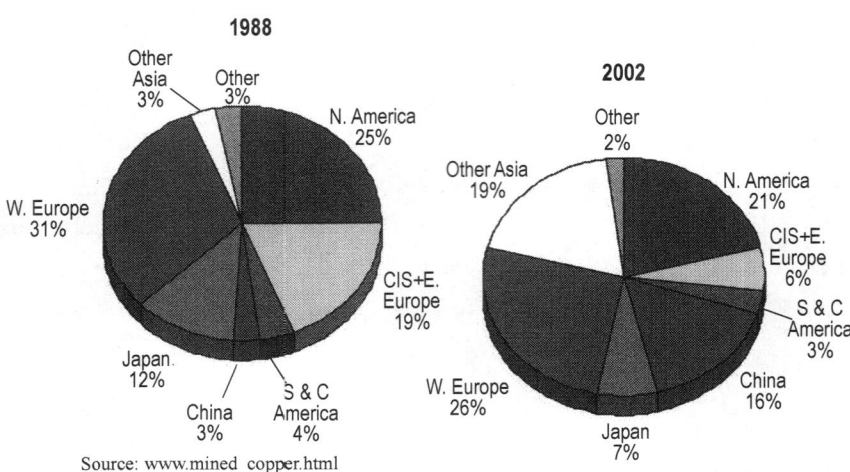

Source: www.mined_copper.html

Although copper production, as well as all non-ferrous metallurgy in Kazakhstan in general, maintains its position in the world market, the reduction in world prices for major metal production has deeply devalued its production profitability. One of the solutions might be the creation of vertically integrated structures (Russian example), in which all process stages, including milling, refining, smelting, production of rolled metal and manufacturing of finished products, are integrated. (Source: Kazakhstan Investment Promotion Center, 2005)

Structure and Strategy of the Copper Industry

The government has a mission to provide a high quality, high world standard copper (99.99% purity), satisfying the needs of shareholders, employees, and customers around the world in an environmentally responsible manner. The copper industry's mission is to direct the industry in all of its activities, including the safety of the environment.

Kazakhmys' strategy is aimed at further transformation of the corporation into a broadly diversified company of world standards, which by its market value and basic financial and economic indicators would match leading international mining and metallurgical firms. In the long term, the corporation intends to raise volumes of production and sales of metals, to develop more efficient technological process stages, to reduce cost of marketable products and maintain its status as the most efficient producer in the world. Industry is heavily invested in re-equipment that allows reducing the losses in the operating processes. In a nutshell, Kazakhmys aims to maintain state-of-the-art technology to produce low-cost, high-quality copper, and to meet international standards for environmental protection and lead the way in operational excellence and safety performance.

The corporate philosophy of Kazakhmys reflects its desire for a fair partnership, realization of the corporation's responsibility to the world and its intention to provide every worker with an opportunity to develop personal abilities and interests. The corporation's success

Figure 6-4
Kazakhstan's Percent of World's Mineral Reserves

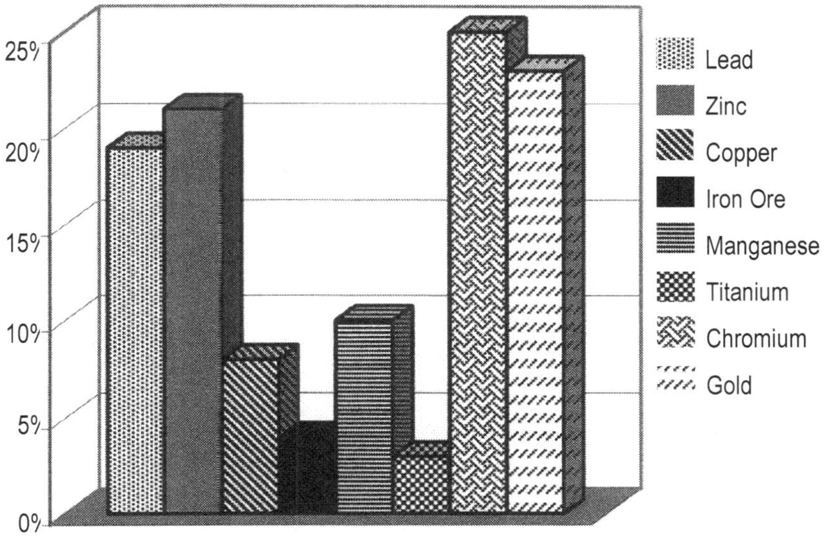

Legend:
Lead, 19%; Zinc, 21%; Copper, 8%; Iron Ore, 4%; Manganese, 10%;
Titanium, 8%; Chromium, 25%; Gold, 10%
Source: www.Minekz.com/mining

is a result of great personal achievements by each employee and good human relations management.

Industry Governance

The decade of independence in the Republic of Kazakhstan has shown that this young Eurasian country has succeeded in overcoming the consequences of the rupture of economic ties within the former Soviet Union, then restored, and even exceeded previous volumes of non-ferrous

Figure 6-5
Breakdown of Kazakhstan's Copper Exports by Country, 1999

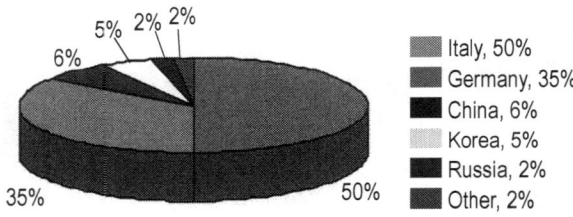

Source: Agency of the Republic of Kazakhstan on Statistics

metal production. Many smaller and medium companies have been consolidated into the growing Kazakhmys Corporation.

Kazakhmys Corporation is the only player in the copper industry. The corporation has consolidated all enterprises of Kazakhstan's copper industry. It includes enterprises of the Zhezkazgan region, the Balkhashsky integrated mining-and-metallurgical mill, the copper smelter and sulfuric acid mill, the Zhezkentsky integrated mining-and-concentrating mill, the Irtishsky and Belousovsky mines, the Berezovskaya and Verkhne-Berezovskaya concentrating mills, and the Irtishsky copper smeltery. The corporation also comprises three high-capacity thermal electric power stations: Zhezkazganskaya, Balkhashskaya and Topar central distribution. Its coal department, Borly, manages the Molodezhny and Kuu-Chekinsky sections in the Karaganda region.

Based on the extract from the register of the securities holders, as of April 18, 2001, the total number of the Kazakhmys Corporation's (considered to be the only player in the copper industry) securities holders was 11,861, of which 17 were legal entities, and 12,021 were private individuals. Following are the owners with more than 5% of the stake of voting shares:

Figure 6-6
Kazakhmys Corporation's Shareholders

Shareholder name and location	Common Shares	Preferred Shares	Stake %
Informatshionno-uchetnyi centre NSE (Almaty)	1,719,037	-	35.0
Samsung Corporation (Seoul, Korea)	1,244,132	-	25.33
Samsung Hong Kong Ltd. (Seoul, Korea)	845,911	-	17.22
Others	611,300	491,153	22.45
Total:	4,420,380	491,153	100.00

Source: www.kazakhmys.kz, Interviewing Managers of Kazakhmys Corporation

South Korea's company Samsung became a strategic partner of Kazakhmys, which was formed on the basis of the scientific and production association Zhezkazgantsvetmet. And so now the main shareholder of Kazakhmys Corporation is Samsung Corporation.

Copper Industry Structure

The copper industry's structure is illustrated in Figure 6-9 with government ministries at the top and the various business divisions underneath Kazakhmys Corporation's top management. The highlight

Figure 6-7
Kazakhstan's Investment in Copper Mining
Investments, $ million

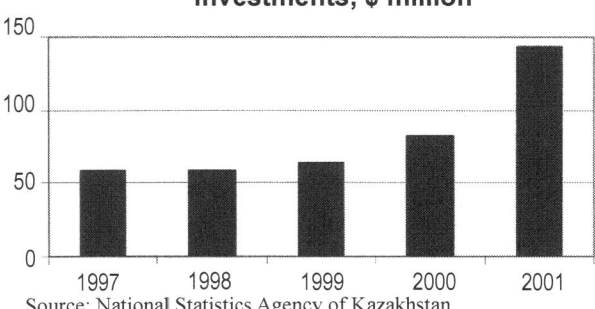

Source: National Statistics Agency of Kazakhstan

112

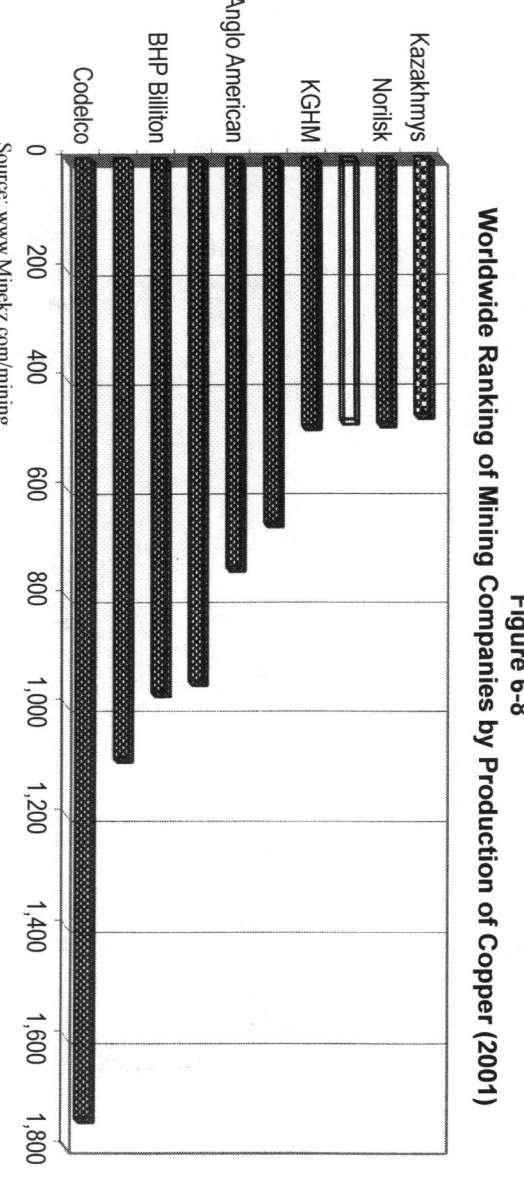

Figure 6-8
Worldwide Ranking of Mining Companies by Production of Copper (2001)

Source: www.Minekz.com/mining

Figure 6-9
Copper Industry Structure

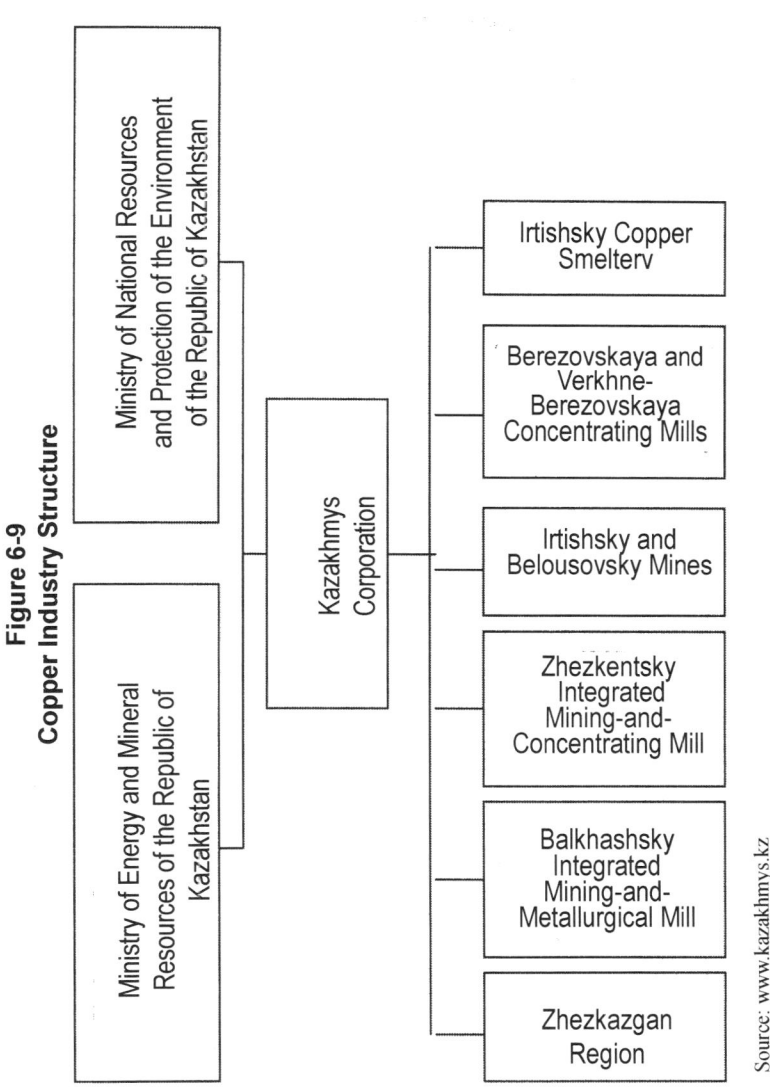

Source: www.kazakhmys.kz

of the corporation's development is its transformation into a vertically integrated and self-sufficient company that enjoys its own coal, electric power, concentrating facilities and three copper smelteries. The large work force (about 70,000 strong) is gradually switching over to Western market ideas with an Eastern corporate philosophy of harmonious development of production and social sphere.

Domestic and International Environments

Kazakhstan's heavily resource-biased industry is one of the major concerns. There are historical roots to this problem–Kazakhstan's economy under the Communist regime was biased towards heavy and mining industries. The Republic developed into a huge resource-base for the Soviet Empire. Although the government is attempting structural reforms in the economy, mineral resource extraction and processing (of metals, for example) represent a major source of budget and export revenues.

Moreover, the extreme volatility of world raw material markets represents a significant danger for investment opportunities. The country's major assets–reserves of oil and metals–are subject to the dramatic price changes in the world markets.

As a consequence of the inherited structure of the national economy, Kazakhstan is characterized by the uneven development of different sectors. Companies in the oil, gas, and metals sectors have experienced higher growth compared to other sectors. Some industries, such as textiles and chemicals, are still in crisis in Kazakhstan.

The government of Kazakhstan supports the copper industry. The Ministry of Energy and Mineral Resources of the Republic of Kazakhstan and the Ministry of National Resources and Protection of the Environment of the Republic of Kazakhstan periodically organize the Kazakhstan International Mining Exploration & Mining Equipment Exhibition. The objective of this high-profile international event is to help realize the unique opportunity to provide all those attending with an updated appraisal of the operational, technical, logistical, and financial issues affecting the Kazakhstan and Central Asian mining and mineral industries.

International organizations also help to develop the copper industry of Kazakhstan. For instance Kazakhstan is involved in the Auselco project (having developed cost-effective solutions for the mineral processing industry throughout Australia, Auselco has shared its experience and expertise with other parts of the world). (Source: Almanac.ods.org/ Kazakhstan, 2005)

To improve environmental standards in Kazakhstan's copper industry, the European Bank for Reconstruction and Development (EBRD) provided a $20 million loan to Kazakhmys Corporation, a major copper processor in the country. The funds have helped Kazakhmys to implement an environmental rehabilitation program for the Balkhash smelter with a goal of achieving World Bank/EU environmental standards.

Providing Kazakhmys access to long-term finance, limited in the industry to date, will enable Kazakhmys to further develop its information systems and production automation systems. Implementation of the environmental program should set a standard for Kazakhmys' other operations, as well as for the industry as a whole. Proceeds of the loan, the Bank's first industrial loan to a locally owned Kazakh company, will also be used for new technology allowing efficient neutralization of sulfur dioxide leading to improvement in the air quality.

The investment climate of Kazakhstan is a very important issue in the copper mining industry. The Constitution of the Republic of Kazakhstan and the Foreign Investment Law provide a series of guarantees designed to protect the interests of foreign investors. These include: (1) the provision of a legal framework for foreign investments, (2) guaranteed use of income at the owner's discretion, (3) guarantees against changes in legislation, (4) guaranteed use of investor's own currency funds, (5) guarantees against expropriation and openness in foreign investors' activity, (6) guarantees against illegal acts of public bodies and officials, (7) guarantees against being checked by the state, and (8) compensation and redress of losses to foreign investors. (Source: Agency of the Republic of Kazakhstan on Investments, 2005)

Figure 6-10
PEST (Political, Economic, Social, Technology)
Analysis of Copper Mining Industry

Political	Economic
• Prior attention from government • Special programs of industry development • Strict government support • Company is monopolist • Mining international exhibitions • International organizations support • One of the main resources of financing economy of Kazakhstan	• One of the important industries in the republic • Large investments • Strong financial position • Geographical expansion • Natural resources is one of priority issues • Economy of Kazakhstan is based on its extensive agricultural and mineral resources • Favorable international market conditions for non-ferrous metals
Social	**Technological**
• Preferences in employment in this sector • Cases of employees' deaths • Low safety techniques • Strong hierarchy • Difficulties with staff promotion • Different training programs • Improvement of labor market conditions	• Low level of technology development • Automatization and computerization • Environment pollution • Production losses during operation & transportation

Opportunities and Threats

Opportunity	Threats
• Increase in demand on international market • Develop infrastructure • Attractive for future investments • Geographical expansion • Government support • New copper recycling technology	• Earthquake • Decrease of price • Unstable economic situation • Decrease of copper consumption • Not keeping pace in new technology • Government limitation • Employees' strikes

Internal Environment Analysis

There are two periods in the copper industry: before 2005, and after 2005 intensive investments.

Figure 6-11
(Before Intensive Investments into Copper Sector)

Strengths	Weaknesses
• 99.99% - pure copper • Low cost in comparison with world competitors • Monopolist • Large reserves of copper • The most recycled metal	• Obsolete technology • Copper losses in operation process and transportation • Supply and demand strongly depend on societal, economic and technological factors • High hierarchy of structure • Poor work conditions for employees • Poor marketing policy

During the period before 2005 (period of less investments), the industry was growing and had a good investment climate. Oil, gas, and mineral resources were development sectors in Kazakhstan and the government itself and other foreign companies found these sectors attractive and competitive on the international market. Even for employees it was a good opportunity to work within these sectors; however, working conditions could have been better (especially in the mining). It is also necessary to

Figure 6-12
(After Intensive Investments into Copper Sector)

Strengths	Weaknesses
• In top 10 in output of copper • Strong base of Kazakhstani economy development • Large reserves of copper • The most recycled metal • Developed infrastructure • Strong financial position • Automatization and computerization • Strong infrastructure • Strong policy of environment protection • Innovative equipment technologies • Near world standards	• Obsolete technology • Supply and demand strongly depend on societal, economic and technological factors • High hierarchy of structure • Poor marketing policy

mention that there was no strong marketing policy in this industry mainly because companies in this industry operated under Business-to-Business relationships.

Concerning the period after 2005, intensive investments did occur which caused improvements in the industry. This sector became very attractive for investors, but still further investments are needed to make Kazakhstan the best supplier of copper in the global market. Even with foreign investments, Kazakhstan faces infrastructural and logistical challenges to cope with foreign competitors. Again, the information systems and computer automation are not equal to the international standards of excellence.

Overview of the Country's Industry Culture

There is no doubt that the investment activity of natural resource users has a positive effect on the social and economical situation in Kazakhstan. These positive factors include: huge revenue increases, increases in local employment, technological development, and development of social and local infrastructure. But there are downsides: pollution and ecological degradation.

The reliance on outdated equipment in most industrial enterprises is a key issue for foreign investors. The situation is especially serious in the power generation and metal industries. Moreover, many companies lack modern technologies and management techniques. However, management contracts in many industrial enterprises, when concessions are given to foreign companies, are expected to improve the situation.

The major issue for foreign investors is the lack of reliable information, primarily financial, on companies that are the object of investment. We would argue that the key problem here is the lack of tradition on information disclosure, and because of: (1) lack of legal requirements and/ or enforcement procedures to protect the rights of minority shareholders, (2) managerial behavior, especially of two major groups of managers– Soviet-style managers and some strategic investors, who sometimes disregard the principles of openness and transparency.

Another key aspect of the problem is methodology. These are the two major issues:

• Accounting standards employed in most enterprises differ from GAAP and/or IAS, although Kazakhstan was the first CIS country to implement a transformation of national accounting standards towards Western principles. To date, just a few companies have completed the modernization of their accounting standards.

• Even fewer companies have completed independent audits according to international standards, and a negligible number of companies have an audit history (audited financial reports covering several years). This is a major precondition for official listing on the Kazakhstan Stock Exchange.

Kazakhmys Corporate Culture

The main characteristics of Kazakhmys corporate culture are: an authoritarian management style, an international team, and 60% local employees and 40% foreign ones.

Taking into account the fact that the company has entered the international market, the corporation can benefit from hiring local staff at the lower level (technical operations), and the top management from foreign countries; therefore, the corporation has incorporated both foreign and domestic personnel in its business activities worldwide. It has resulted in the creation of a multinational team. However, it could create problems of cross-cultural relations. Because of cooperation with different partners such as China, Germany, and Iran, the company could face challenges to manage cross-cultural problems.

Kazakhmys' Profile: Internal Resources

Kazakhmys Corporation is located in Karaganda and in the Eastern-Kazakhstan region of the republic. The majority of enterprises including the head office are located in Zhezkazgan with 12 mines of underground and open-pit extraction, 8 enriching plants, 3 brass works, a copper rod producing plant, some repair and engineering works, a private railway, the road and air transport fleet, shaft construction and mounting trusts, 2 open-pit mines, and 3 heating power stations. The representative office is in Astana, which is the capital of Kazakhstan. Its principal activities are: Mining, refining and processing of non-ferrous ores; Copper production; Gold and silver refining; Chemical production; Power generation; and Coal mining.

Kazakhmys Corporation has the following administrative entities: Enterprises in the Zhezkazgan region, the Balkhash Mining Metallurgical Combine, VostokKazmed, the Department of Power Stations, the Coal Department "Borly," the Karaganda Foundry, and the Karaganda Machine-Building Foundry.

The enterprises in the Zhezkazgan Region are: 4 underground mines and 1 open mine extracting 26 ml. ton. of ore per year; a Mine development trust; 3 concentrators with an annual capacity of 26 ml. ton.; 1 copper smelter with 250,000 t. copper cathode annual output; a Copper Wire Rod Plant; a Power Station; a Scientific Research Institute; an Industrial Railway Transport Enterprise; 2 Specialized Repairing Plants; a Construction Trust; and Infrastructure.

Balkhash Mining Metallurgical Combine units are: Kounrad, Sayak and Shatyrkol open mines; Concentrator; Copper Smelter; Chemical Metallurgical Combine (precious metals refinery and zinc plant).

VostokKazmed units include: a Copper Chemical Combine, which is located in Ust-Talovka village at a distance of 100 km from the regional center of Eastern Kazakhstan-Ust-Kamenogorsk city; Zhezkent Mining Combine, which is located in Eastern Kazakhstan at a distance of 230 km from its regional center-Ust-Kamenogorsk city; 2 underground mines (Belousovka village); 2 concentrators (Belousovka village).

The Department of Power Stations consists of: the chief distributing power station which is located at a distance of 60 km from Karaganda city; the Zhezkazgan and Balkhash power stations. Total electric capacity—500 MWt, total heating capacity—435 HCal/h, annual power generation is over 2 bl. 800 ml. kWt/h.

Coal Department "Borly" units: Kuu-Chekinskyi and Molodezhnyi

Figure 6-13
Characteristics of Kazakhmys' Sites

Name of Site	Type of Ore	Size of Site	Approximate Reserves Sufficiency, Years
Central Kazakhstan			
Jezkazgan	Copper ore	Large	20
Jylandy group of sites	Copper ore	Large	15
Jaman – Aibat	Copper ore	Large	34
Kounradskoe	Copper ore	Large	21
Sayak –1	Copper ore	Small	10
Tastau	Copper ore	Small	7
Kuu-Chekinskoe	Coal	Small	14
Borlinskoe	Coal	Small	113
Eastern Kazakhstan			
Orlovskoe	Polymetallic ores	Large	20
Nikolaevskoe	Polymetallic ores	Small	10
Shemonaikhinkoe	Polymetallic ores	Small	15
Artemievskoe	Polymetallic ores	Small	21
Belousovskoe	Polymetallic ores	Small	17
Irtyshskoe	Polymetallic ores	Small	22
Yiubileino-Snegirikhskoe	Polymetallic ores	Small	20
South Kazakhstan			
Skalnoe	Construction material	Small	
Aktas-3	Fluxing limestone	Small	23
Belokamennoe	Marble	Small	
Jatyrkol	Copper-molybdenum	Average	8 years of open mining

Source: www.Kazakhmys.kz

coal pits with annual capacity of 7 ml. ton and Nukazgan copper deposit (projected annual capacity - 4 ml. ton).

Karaganda Foundry produces milling balls for Kazakhmys concentrators.

Karaganda Machine-Building Foundry produces different equipment and hydraulic systems for Kazakhmys underground mines. The production is fully based on its own raw material base (37.4m tons of ore a year). Kazakhmys also has licenses to develop 23 sites with copper, polymetallic mines, construction materials, and coal. Mining geological formations of the ores allow the corporation to develop sites for both open-pit and underground mining. The ore reserves for some of the sites under the current production level are sufficient for about 34 years.

Kazakhmys is engaged in a complete production cycle, beginning from the extraction to production of finished goods. The corporation produces copper, zinc concentrates, cathode copper, wire rods, rare metals, sulfuric acid, coal, and generates electricity and heat. From 1995 to 2000 production and the processing of ores increased as much as three-fold. In the last 5 years, the following were accomplished: Annenskii mine (4m tons of ore a year), Itauz pit at Jylandy site (2m tons a year), 73/75 mine (2m tons a year). In 2000 Shatyrkol mine was put into service. The gold and silver refinery plant and enamel covered wire production plant in Balkhash were put into service. To restore the reserves of copper mining, work was done at the Jaman-Aibat (copper), Artemievskoe and Orlovskoe (polymetallic) sites.

Being a joint stock company, Kazakhmys was the first to use xanthogen (a chemical used in ore concentration) in Kazakhstan and it will supply it to all of its plants. Within Kazakhstan the company is the leader in the volume of non-ferrous and precious metals production.

The most important projects are: The mines at Zhaman-Aibat, Shatyrkol, and Nurkazgan; the development of down horizons of the Zhezkazgan deposit (the mine Annensky, the shaft # 73/75, 70), and up horizons of the mine at Artemeyvskyi.

Figure 6-14
Output of Pure Copper by
Kazakhmys' Enterprises
(Thousands tons)

Year	Output, Thousand tons
1997	301.0
1998	324.5
1999	361.9
2000	394.7
2001	481.4
2005	572.5

Source: Adapted from www.kazakhmys.kz

The major research and development works are: The development and introduction of the rational technology of double extraction; the creation of a new system for the extraction of the mine stock and its management by a bigger layer of mine in order to avoid the accumulation of the emptiness, the way of open development, the introduction of a financial IT system "Platinum SQL," and, the introduction of an atomized system "the management of mountain-mine equipment." The results of these sets of actions include: A number of protective measures were implemented in the course of the reconstruction of vitriol workshops; Mine water treatment facilities were installed; Upgrading of dust-catching plants.

In cooperation with scientists from the Kazakh State Academy of Science, it has developed an innovative and conceptually a new product. The name is "L23." There is no analogue of this innovation among the CIS market, it is a unique product.

Copper Industry Operations and Logistics

The geological mining conditions of Kazakhstan on the bedding of ore bodies permits the development of the deposits by open and underground methods.

Most modern copper mining is done in open pits with explosives, giant shovels, and huge trucks to haul the ore to a mill or smelter. Exploration and development require the careful extraction of rock samples to determine ore content. When a site is identified as containing significant ore content, it is prepared for mining. Moving materials: Rocks are blasted to break them into smaller pieces and loaded into large trucks for transport to one of two processing locations. Where the ore goes–either to concentrating and smelting, or to leaching and electro-winning–depends on how much copper and the types of minerals it contains.

Development rock is the material that must be excavated to access the ore. Milling: In one copper production process, rock that comes from the mine is crushed into smaller and smaller pieces by heavy steel balls in machinery called mills. Concentrating: ground up rock is mixed with water, air bubbles and small amounts of chemicals. The chemicals allow the copper minerals to rise to the top and stick to floating air bubbles. The remaining mixture of crushed rock and water–called tailing–separates from the copper-bearing bubbles. The copper minerals are skimmed off and dried to form copper concentrate, a powder-like material. Smelting: In the smelter, copper concentrate is melted and copper is separated from other substances in the concentrate. Molten copper is poured into molds called anodes. The unwanted material cools to a glass-like substance called slag. The natural metals that remain in slag are sorted out.

In an alternate copper production process, as a first step called leaching, rock is taken from the mine directly to stockpiles. A solution of slightly acidic water is dripped on the stockpiles, percolating down through the rock and dissolving copper along the way. The solution containing the copper is collected and piped to holding ponds. Solution Extraction and Electro-winning: In tanks, the copper-bearing solution is mixed with chemicals that transfer the copper to a more concentrated solution called electrolyte. The electrolyte is pumped to steel tanks. Starter sheets hang in the solution and, using an electric current, the copper is plated from the electrolyte onto the sheet, forming 99.99 percent pure copper plates. All solutions used during this process are recycled.

Kazakhmys can boast of its own automobile, railroad and air transport as well as up-to-date information networks, technological telecommunications systems, and skilled personnel. (All these enterprises were mentioned above.) All these are components of Kazakhmys' success. In its natural state, copper is found mixed with numerous minerals and this gives rise to the following classification: native copper, sulfured minerals and oxidized minerals. Apart from these natural sources (known as primary copper), there is also copper scrap (secondary copper). Scrap is another example of the metal's qualities, as is the ease with which it can be recovered from old buildings, from electrical equipment and obsolete facilities, and from old pieces of metal, allowing scrap to become an important method of supply on the international market. In the copper industry we see a quasi-privatization at work in the post-Soviet Republic of Kazakhstan.

Policy Implications for Kazakhstan

The major copper mines are located in the Balkhash Complex, the Eastern Region, and the Zhezkazgan Complex; investments and support for the copper industry are both domestic and foreign. ABN AMRO Bank Kazakhstan, Future Kapital, various governments including Kazakhstan, and Samsung Company are stake holders in Kazakhmys Corporation. In the copper industry, we see a quasi-privatization at work in the post-Soviet Republic of Kazakhstan. There are management challenges facing Kazakhmys: logistics, infrastructure, information systems, technology, and others. To mitigate these issues, Kazakhmys should engage in modernizing its equipment, technology, human resources, infrastructure, logistics, and information technology. These are vital to sustain growth and remain competitive in world markets.

Figure 6-15
Map of Copper and Other Minerals in Kazakhstan

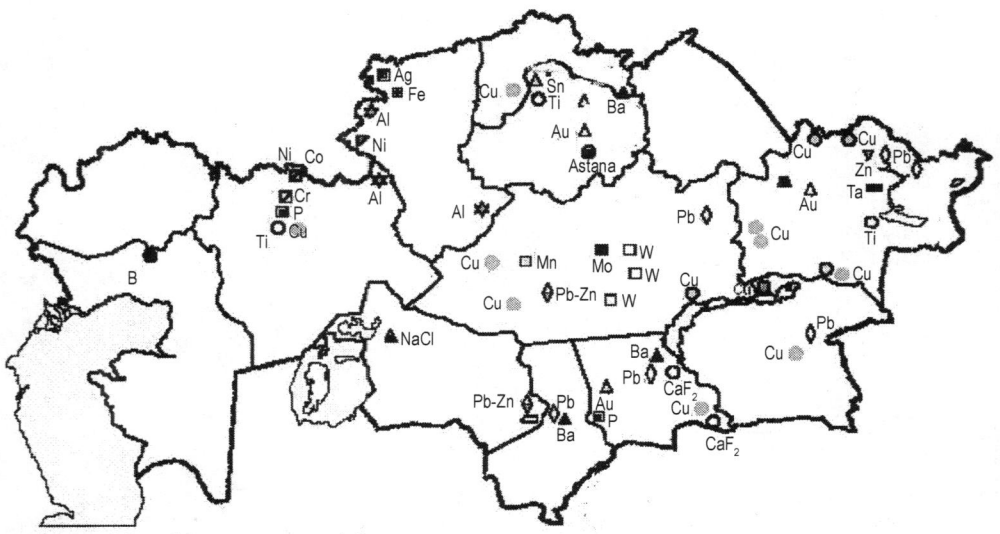

Source: Adapted from www.copperinfo.com

Legend:
Cu = Copper   B = Boron   Ti = Titanium   P = Phosphorus
Co = Cobalt   Al = Aluminum   Fe = Iron   Ag = Silver
Ba = Barium   Cr = Chromium   Ni = Nickel

Chapter 7

The Construction Industry: Internationalization and Growth

Introduction

Changes in Kazakhstan's economy are presenting new challenges to the construction industry. The ability of construction companies to respond to them will have significant implications for the industry.

This chapter provides insights into the construction industry in Kazakhstan. There are four major segments into which the construction industry can be divided: the social segment, the manufacturing segment, the transportation and communications segment, and the shop and service segment. The social segment consists of the following sub-segments: home infrastructure, education infrastructure, government infrastructure, healthcare infrastructure, and others. The manufacturing segment includes heavy manufacturing and light manufacturing. The transportation and communications segment consists of the following sub-segments: auto, rail, pipelines, telecommunications, and air transport. The shop and service segment includes retail shops, repair shops, hotels, and other services.

On December 16, 1991, the Republic of Kazakhstan declared its independence. Chaos ensued in the economy. On January 5, 1992, President Nazarbayev removed price controls, and markets were opened. Western products flooded the market; local manufacturing stopped and the construction industry declined further in most of Kazakhstan except in the western oil regions.

127

Before August 19, 1998, that is, before the Russian economic crisis, the western oil regions fueled Kazakhstan's oil industry and related construction projects. In other regions of Kazakhstan, plants were closed, especially those that supplied Russian plants with "Soviet products." Kazakhstan's growth, which was adversely affected by the Russian financial crisis of August 1998, declined from 1998 to 2000 (See Figure 7-1).

Figure 7-1
Construction Growth in Eurasian Countries

	In % from previous year			
	1997	1998	1999	2000
Kazakhstan	112	142	122	138
Russia	65	93	105	118
Azerbaijan	167	145	98	102
Belarus	120	116	92	97
Georgia	187	200	43	102
Kyrgyzstan	65	47	98	104
Moldova	94	100	79	101
Uzbekistan	117	115	102	101
Ukraine	93	105	100	111

Source: National Statistics Agency of Kazakhstan

Statistics, Strategy, and Scope of the Industry

Over 7,100 legal entities operate in the construction industry, including 193 state-owned and 6,875 private firms. The construction industry provides a favorable investment climate for foreign investors. There are 153 joint ventures with foreign firms and 102 enterprises (with 100% foreign capital) operating as affiliates. Most of the main industrial enterprises in this sector have been transferred into foreign management. Almost all industrial enterprises and organizations in the construction industry have been privatized in accordance with the state privatization program.

Certainly, the country's general economic situation affected the construction industry. The effect was indicated by a reduction in the construction sector's share of GDP, from 12% in 1990 to 4.2% in 1997.

The construction materials industry's share of GDP also fell from 5.6% to 2.2%. However, investments in the construction industry are bringing about a fast turnaround in this situation. Construction projects in Astana and in some key sectors (petrochemicals, metallurgy, and the mining industry) are attracting foreign investment. However, the volume of foreign investment in development within the construction materials industry needs to be increased.

Much like the entire economy of Kazakhstan, the construction sector is very dependent on the success or failure of the oil industry. The direct demands of the oil companies include construction work in the oil fields, as well as office buildings in the capital. There are also several infrastructure projects in the country directed toward the needs of this sector—for instance, the new oil port in Aktau. The interest in oil has also meant an increased need for banks, hotels, and other buildings in businesses servicing the oil companies. The move of the administrative capital from Almaty to Astana has also meant business opportunities for construction companies.

The main opportunities are in the area of engineering services for the construction of facilities relating to oil and gas (offshore and onshore field development, transport pipelines, oil refining, gas processing, and petrochemicals), notably in relation to the development of the huge fields of Tengiz, Karachaganak, and Kashagan. However, while the oil and gas sector will be the major purchaser of architecture, construction, and engineering services for years to come, there is demand for these services throughout this developing country.

There is a growing demand for all types of construction services: construction, renovation, and conservation of industrial and public utilities and residential buildings, and design and assembly services. There is a need for a full range of civil engineering, construction, and engineering activities that include the following: research and development, all aspects of design, design and build, management contracting, construction management, turnkey projects, partnering and PFI, tunneling, foundation engineering, and mining and facilities management.

Many opportunities exist in the continuing expansion of the new capital city, Astana, and in strengthening and diversifying the country's infrastructure. There are plans for upgrading, expanding or building new ports, airports, roads, and power distribution grids. President Nazarbayev declared Astana Kazakhstan's new capital in 1997 and the government completed its move there in 2000. The government has proceeded with ambitious plans to build up the area between Astana's city center and the airport. The rapid growth of Astana, especially the growth of new administrative buildings and housing, demands the development of social and service infrastructure.

A special development program for the attraction of direct investments has been successfully implemented. The volume of the program is $130 million. During the year 2002, at a cost of $98 million, there were eighty buildings (shops, cafes, etc.) already built and functioning. Besides this, in accordance with the city development program and detailed layout plans, a working schedule was adopted for the construction of transportation and communications infrastructure. Projects included the following: upgrading the Almaty-Astana motorway (900 kilometers); construction of a circular roadway around Astana; reconstruction of the Astana Airport; construction of business centers, a trade center, and Western-standard hotels; and residential construction. Turkey has been very active, with more than ten Turkish construction firms operating in the country.

To stimulate investment, the government granted tax holidays to companies investing in housing and public utilities construction in Astana. Those investors will be exempt from paying income tax, land tax, and property tax for up to five years. The construction industry serving Astana is growing quickly, and construction materials for Astana and its outlying regions are in short supply. Typically, the tender process for construction projects is not transparent, so U.S. companies are advised to watch for tender announcements financed by multilateral institutions such as the European Bank for Reconstruction and Development (EBRD), and the Asian Development Bank (ADB). EBRD and ADB have granted loans to facilitate the rehabilitation of the Almaty-Bishkek road (245km) and to finance small-scale improvements to access roads. An ADB loan

Figure 7-2
Breakdown of Kazakhstani Investments in Construction
(in thousands of dollars)

By Province	1997	1998	1999	2000
Akmola *(excluding Astana city)*	1,008	2,016	914	1,445
Aktube	8,138	14,952	16,052	7,178
Almaty *(excluding Almaty city)*	6,373	9,046	8,913	7,178
Atyrau	33,176	55,118	68,165	98,052
Zhambyl	2,035	1,540	1,672	1,330
Karaganda	9,207	14,160	10,872	17,636
Kysylorda	4,787	7,057	10,229	5,141
Kostanay	5,059	4,781	4,950	9,359
Mangystau	13,424	16,798	8,056	29,695
Pavlodar	5,502	7,211	3,232	1,968
Major Cities				
Almaty	12,333	13,933	10,493	11,951
Astana	19,273	37,222	50,060	45,707
By region				
Western region	59,903	94,930	146,052	1,135,766
Northern region	16,911	23,448	19,968	30,426
Eastern region	14,894	23,338	19,905	31,618
Southern region	16,476	21,622	23,544	24,363

Source: National Statistics Agency of Kazakhstan

worth $52 million and an EBRD loan worth $25.5 million was spent on reconstructing the Almaty-Bishkek road in 2003-04.

The need for construction materials provides another opportunity for U.S. companies. Only 47% of the construction materials used in Kazakhstan is available domestically. Locally produced materials include cement, bricks, wooden doors, windows, steel doors, and soft and iron roofs. All other materials are imported from Turkey, China, and Germany.

Mission and Strategic Objectives

The industry's mission is to ensure development of the construction sector for stable economic growth and improvement of living standards in Kazakhstan. The strategic objectives for development of the construction sector include the establishment of a high-grade market for housing and public utility services and design and contract services, and the modernization and technical re-equipment of industrial facilities. The realization of these strategic objectives involves: (1) the implementation of financial and investment policies to ensure favorable conditions in the investment environment; (2) the improvement in pricing policies in the construction industry; (3) the improvement of architectural and urban development control; (4) the reform of design and research service organizations; and (5) interstate cooperation in the field of construction. Those objectives are consistent with the mission and with the internal and external environments.

Figure 7-3
Sources of Financing for Commercial Construction
(In millions of dollars)

	1997	1998	1999	2000
Government Budget funds	6.9	11.8	9.7	9.2
Private Corporate Funds	67.8	56.9	46.8	53.5
Individuals	3.5	2.2	2.1	1.6
Foreign funds	21.8	29.1	41.4	35.7

Source: National Statistics Agency of Kazakhstan

These strategies also include the revitalization of manufacturing and the realization of particular investment projects concerned with the modernization of existing facilities in the housing construction sector and the development of a design service market. The construction industry policies imply the production and consumption of high quality materials that are used in accordance with ISO standards. The current mission, objectives, policies, and strategies reflect the industry's operations. Latest trends in the economy of Kazakhstan are consistent with the above-mentioned issues. The Ministry of Industries and Trade governs the construction sector.

External Environment

Political stability and the continuing development of the Kazakhstani economy in 2001 resulted in the growth of incomes and a boom for the construction market. Recovering from the financial crisis and tenge devaluation of 1998, the construction sector has been steady since then. This is explained by the growing incomes of the middle class, who are purchasing more and more apartments. Changes in the current economy in the past decade have been presenting new challenges to the construction industry. The ability of construction companies to respond to them will mean significant opportunities for other businesses.

The following trends are affecting the industry. Economic and population growth, along with increasing income, have created a huge demand for construction. Kazakhstan's economy is very dependent on the energy sector, that is, the oil and gas industry's vulnerability to oil price fluctuation, as well as new reserves discovery. Also, the investment climate in the construction industry depends on foreign investments, which help to develop the infrastructure. The war in Iraq is a threat. Kazakhstan could lose foreign investments that are necessary for the further development of its oil reserves. Strong development of the housing construction industry was reached due to the efforts of the National Bank of Kazakhstan and the government, which have been encouraging commercial banks to offer more housing credit. The numbers of banking and non-banking organizations which drive mortgage lending demand have been growing. New types of mortgage loans have been implemented. The terms of lending have been growing longer, and the rates on loans have been going down.

Technological forces are presenting opportunities for the industry;

new construction technologies and advanced materials appear on the market. Accordingly, leading construction companies implement these technologies that were designed outside the country.

Political-legal aspects are regulated by the government, which protects local construction companies by establishing standards, quotas, and tender requirements. The law limits foreign participation in "joint construction ventures," imposes new requirements on the use of subcontractors, and sets procedures for state and public control over construction activities.

Socio-culturally, the population density of the cities is one of the factors that determine the development of the construction sector. The growth of middle and higher levels of income ensures construction sector prosperity. The average income per capita increased by 113.7% in 2002 over the year before, and by 114.3% in 2003.

The external factors influencing the industry are different throughout the country mostly due to economic and political issues. For example, Atyrau and Aktau are the richest and most rapidly developing regions in Kazakhstan due to oil and gas exploration there. These cities are the closest and most convenient region for the transportation of goods—especially by using the less expensive means of river and sea transportation. There are obvious signs of revitalization in the construction industry. The move of the administrative capital from Almaty to Astana has also meant business opportunities for the construction companies. Although most of the official buildings are in place by now, there still is a need for modern offices and housing in the new capital in the middle of the Kazakh steppes.

Figure 7-4
Construction Industry Revenues through the Years

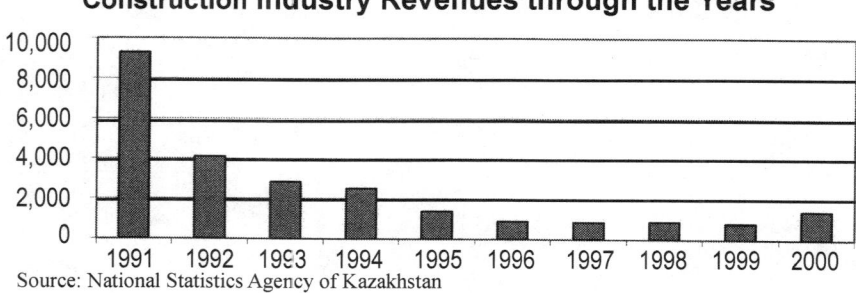

Source: National Statistics Agency of Kazakhstan

Figure 7-5
Construction Industry Economic Indicators
(in millions of dollars)

	2000	2001	2002	2003
Construction materials industry volume of output at the comparable wholesale rates of 1997	183.2	287.8	468.8	793.1
Investment in housing construction	234.5	1,519.3	2,331.3	2,649.1
Government capital investment in housing construction	6.3	5.1	4.2	0.6
Government Scientific and technical development	0.87	1	0.71	0.47
Foreign industrial construction investments	109	151.2	196.6	422.5

Source: National Statistics Agency of Kazakhstan

Industry Analysis

Kazakhstan's construction market has been slightly expanded and rejuvenated, with a trend away from public provision to private sector construction.

The entry barriers to Kazakhstan's construction markets are not high. The main barrier is the reputation that the companies have established. The reputation or corporate image that any existing company enjoys in the construction market is a key competitive advantage. With the current development of economic globalization, more and more foreign companies will enter Kazakhstan's construction market. These multinational companies are either from developed countries (e.g., Italy, Turkey, and Bulgaria) or from emerging countries (e.g., Uzbekistan). They each have some competitive advantages, in terms of technology, management skill, or capital—as well as cost. This will constitute a serious threat to existing Kazakhstani companies.

The buyers in the construction industry have some characteristics that are different from other industries. First, the buyers, the owners of the project, initiate the project, and they will award the project through open tender to the company they assume will do the best job. This gives the buyers a lot of bargaining power over construction companies. Second, every project in which a construction company takes part usually lasts long enough to contribute a very important part of the revenues of that company. This means the potential for any company to get new projects will have a great effect on its profitability ... and even its survival. This puts the construction companies at a disadvantage. Third, with so many small companies now active in the Kazakhstani construction market, with technical or service abilities being equal, this gives the buyers many more choices. Fourth, the buyers have no switching costs; they can just decide between contractors based on their own strategies.

With the development of the economy, the needs of the customers also have been changing. This leads to changes in the bargaining powers among them. The increasingly technical and procedural complexity of the projects requires the construction companies' active participation in all phases of the projects.

Building materials manufacturing is characterized by the dominance of large firms. A small number of large publicly listed firms dominate the market. That can put a construction engineering company, especially a smaller company, in a weaker position. The construction industry could be currently described as follows: rivalry is high (e.g. Bazis-A, ElitStroi, Kuat, MAK, Astana-finance—in residential construction); threat of potential entrants is moderate; bargaining power of suppliers is low; bargaining power of buyers is high; and government regulations and human rights concerns are growing. The industry sustains a high overall growth rate.

In the residential construction industry, the five largest companies (Bazis-A, ElitStroi, Kuat, MAK, and Astana-finance) account for nearly 30% of industry volume. Also, there are many small firms active in this business; market share based on housing value indicates that a small minority of volume builders and a group of medium-sized firms have market dominance. The large number of small firms in the industry decides the instability within the industry because they are relatively balanced in terms of size and perceived resources, and they are prone to fight each other in order to gain projects. On the other hand, the dominance of the large firms may lead to stability because they can impose discipline as well as play a coordinative role in the industry. All this causes complexity in the relationships among competitors in Kazakhstan's construction industry. The bargaining power of buyers is the most critical issue for the industry at present. With the development of the economy, the needs as well as lifestyle orientation of the customers also have been changing. The worsening demographic situation and migration outflow may adversely impact the whole industry. The industry is immature with a high growth rate. Based on current trends in each of these competitive forces, the industry appears to be increasing in its level of competitive intensity.

Marketing

In 2002, the government of Kazakhstan allocated 133 billion tenge ($867 million at the official exchange rate) for construction projects of national importance. There are no reliable statistics for the private sector, but construction officials and experts add another 40% ($348 million) for medium and small-scale construction projects and private-sector construction. This makes the total construction sector figure $1.2 billion (including construction materials, services, and equipment). In 2001, all local construction companies carried out construction and assembly work for 338.85 billion tenge ($2.2 billion). According to official data, in the first half of 2002, the construction spending by the government grew by 3.5%.

Overview of Industry Segments

Floor-space segment. Generally, people in Kazakhstan prefer living in private houses. However, those who cannot afford a house live in apartments, in four- to nine-story buildings. Construction of residential buildings is the responsibility of the local government (akimats).

138

Figure 7-6
Number of Construction Companies through the Years

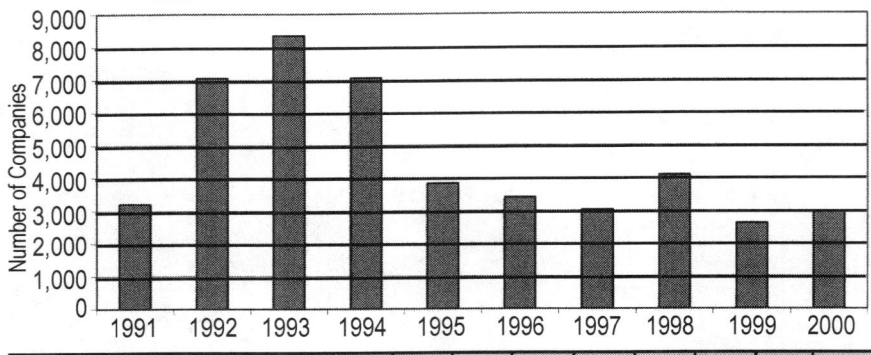

	1991	1992	1993	1994	1995	1996	1997	1998	1999	2000
Industry Revenue, (millions of Tenge)	9292	4098	2833	2512	1371	879	846	889	790	1409
Number of Companies	3200	7056	8344	7056	3820	3399	3019	4072	2610	2967

Source: National Statistics Agency of Kazakhstan

Figure 7-7
Ratio of State to Private Construction Companies

Year	2000	2001
State companies, %	29.4	28.1
Private companies, %	70.6	71.9

Almaty city akimat is the main customer of Bazis-A, the largest private construction company in Kazakhstan.

Large governmental enterprises such as KazakhTelecom, the Ministry of Internal Affairs, the Ministry of Foreign Economic Relations, the Ministry of Defense, and others, opt to build apartments for their own employees. In such cases, the ministry or agency selects the construction company itself. Experience shows that, being one of the largest construction companies in the republic, Bazis-A gets the majority of orders. But other companies, both local and foreign, are also eligible to participate in these construction projects.

Total floor space in Kazakhstan is 590.6 million square meters, of which 323.8 million square meters are in urban areas; the remaining 266.8

million square meters are in rural areas. The housing sector consists of 5.7 million apartments or individual houses, of which 5.4 million are private apartments and houses and the remaining 0.3 million apartments and houses are government-owned. Fully 90% of the population lives in their own apartments or houses.

In urban areas, 6% of houses were built before 1950, 43% between 1950 and 1970, 29% between 1971 and 1980, and the remaining 22% were built after the year 1980. In rural areas, construction of residences developed faster: 3% of houses and apartments were built before 1950, 42% were built between 1951 and 1970; the remaining 55% were built over the last 25 years. So, the repair and redesign construction market has great potential for this segment.

Non-industrial construction segment. Large national projects (such as the parliament building, Almaty city International Airport, and the President's Hall) are usually accompanied by special government decrees and funding from the state budget, as well as a hard currency budget. The large state construction companies usually participate in this type of construction project. For interior work, the government announces a tender for foreign companies. Turkish construction companies are very active in Kazakhstan's construction market. They bring technologies, skilled workers, construction materials, and specialized tools for interior work.

Tenders are announced in different ways. Sometimes they are announced through newspapers, and sometimes companies are contacted directly. Bids on tenders for construction projects are usually sent to those foreign construction companies which have representative offices in Astana or Almaty city. This generally means that company representatives know how to do business in Kazakhstan, and are aware of all the advantages and disadvantages of being in Kazakhstan's construction market.

Industrial construction segment. Special construction companies usually carry out industrial projects such as plants, refineries, power stations, and dams. For example, Kazhydrostroy will build a water purification plant with funding coming from the Ministry of Agriculture, while Kazenergospetsstroy will build a power station funded by the Ministry of Energy. However, large projects, either of national importance in a new industrial sector or to be built with foreign investment, will generally attract foreign construction companies.

The following projects are considered desirable for foreign investors' participation. Projects in water supply construction are planned and implemented by the Ministry of Agriculture; the main contractor is Kazhydrostroy. These projects involve reclamation of new land and complex reconstruction of old irrigated land; improvement of the ecological situation in the Aral Sea basin; and construction of interregional, inter-district, main, and street water supplies. Major parts of projects in transportation and communications are planned and implemented by Kazakhstan Railways State Company (Kazakhstan Temir Joly). The main contractor is the association Kaztransstroy and the major activities are expansion of road and communications networks and improvement of their quality, electrification of operating railways, and construction of a new metro line.

Private estate construction segment. With the development of Kazakhstan's economy, the middle and upper classes have risen, especially in the finance-intensive cities of Almaty and Astana. For example, the number of households in Almaty increased from 453,000 in 1996 to 895,000 in 2002. The demand for quality construction services has become more apparent. The private construction market is in a growth stage, and the rivalry among private construction companies inside the segment is intense.

Overview of Key Competitors

According to the Ministry of Macroeconomics and Statistics, the ratio of state to private companies in the civil construction sector was 29.4% (state) to 70.6% (private) in 2000, and 28.1% (state) to 71.9% (private) in 2001 (see Figure 7-7).

The state sector. The state sector is mostly administered by former state construction ministries (such as the Ministry of Construction and the Ministry of Transport and Communications) that have been reformed into so-called private joint stock associations/concerns/corporations, many of which are, in fact, 35-50% state-owned. Each entity is responsible for construction in a different area:

Almatykyrylys Corporation is the biggest in Almaty city, and one of the biggest in Kazakhstan. The corporation is responsible for industrial and residential construction projects in Almaty city. Kazagrostroy Association is responsible for construction in rural areas. Funding comes from local (regional) governments. Kaztransstroy Association is responsible for the construction and repair of railways, roads, metro lines, trolley-bus and tram lines in cities, tunnels, bridges, buildings associated with transportation (such as railway repair shops, and railway and metro car manufacturing and repair plants), electrification of all existing railways, and the construction of railways and roads going to large factories in Kazakhstan.

Kazhydrostroy Concern is involved in the construction of channels, collectors, water plants, land irrigation and reclamation systems, pumping stations, and water supply systems in rural areas. This company usually works in steppe and desert areas. Its second objective is to construct adjoining buildings and infrastructure such as roads, residences, schools, clinics, and nursery schools.

Kazhydroenergostroy Association is a department of the Ministry of Energy and Electrification. The association is responsible for building hydropower stations and dams. Currently there is no funding for the construction of new stations or dams, or reconstruction of existing ones. All construction concerns and associations generally work on turnkey conditions. Their departments and divisions are responsible for the design, utilities (gas and water pipelines, electrical wiring, and sewage systems), and roads. There are special divisions within these concerns and associations that are responsible for procurement. These concerns produce most of the construction materials they use in their own firms.

Civil construction sector. The civil construction sector in Kazakhstan consists of local private companies as well as foreign companies. Foreign companies usually bring their own construction equipment and tools. Some of them have permanent representative offices in the country. Many companies are in the country only on a temporary basis for the duration of their construction project.

Most local companies are small, usually only employing 20-25 people. These companies are young and do not have sufficient funds to buy construction equipment. There are only two large local construction companies, which are real leaders in the local market. They are Elitstroy and Bazis-A. There are several private construction materials production companies. All of them are involved in interior materials production such as doors, windows, bathtubs, and bathroom items.

Marketing Objectives, Strategies, and Policies of Bazis-A

Bazis-A's portfolio includes constructing standard large-panel multi-story houses and small office buildings as well as specially designed buildings utilizing the newest technologies and materials. Bazis-A is considered the prime mover in the industry and stands out from all its competition.

The current trends in the Almaty construction market, as well as changes in the external environment, have made marketing a critically important tool for generating increased sales. The bargaining power of the customers has strengthened as they have stiffened their requirements for better quality and a more sophisticated product mix. Bazis-A's performance is also dependent on industry factors such as increased competition, as well as technological issues.

Bazis-A has the following marketing objectives: a high rate of market penetration, retention of current customers, an increase in brand awareness, brand extension, constant development and updating of the product mix, increased levels of advertising and promotion, and attracting government orders. The financial objectives of Bazis-A are to increase market share by 3% every year, and to decrease cost-of-goods-sold/sales to 85% before 2007.

The corporate objectives are consistent with those of the industry as a whole and with the external and internal environments. Despite the changing external factors and fierce competition, every regional business unit of Bazis-A has increased sales and market share in the local markets. The company operates in Almaty, Astana, Atyrau, Aktau, Taldy-Kurgan, and Pavlodar.

In 1998, the volume of investments in capital construction by large and mid-sized enterprises totaled $2,035.3 million. In comparable dollars, this is 39% more than in 1997; $941.2 million was invested in fixed assets. About 36% of the fixed assets were invested in manufacturing industry enterprises, 19% in mining, and 16% in housing construction. About 41% of the investments were committed to housing construction and renovation. The mining and processing industry, as well as transportation and communications attracted 42%, 14%, and 12% of the total volume of investments respectively, for the creation and reproduction of fixed capital in these sectors. Foreign investments in these activities were 38%, 26%, and 22%, respectively. The volume of investment attracted for the construction of education and agriculture facilities was relatively insignificant.

Non-financial corporations are providing significant investment in the construction industry. In 1998, their investments in capital construction totaled approximately $1,823.5 million (90% of the country's volume), whereas financial corporations and official bodies invested only an insignificant share, $43.5 million (2%) and $108.2 million (5%). At the same time, private householders invested $51.8 million (3%).

Most national and local budgets were directed toward the construction and reconstruction of state enterprises (97%). An insignificant share of these investments (3%) was distributed among private enterprises and organizations, involved in the construction of housing foundations, air transportation, oil and gas production, steam and water supply facilities, the chemical and automobile industries, and stock-breeding facilities. The share of local government budgets within the total volume of capital construction investments, considered regionally, is the highest in these oblasts: Kzyl-Orda (26%), South Kazakhstan (19%), and Kostanai (13%).

The share of construction investment financed by the state budget was highest in the Northern Kazakhstan oblast (44% of the total regional investment volume) and in Astana (50%). The share of foreign investments in fixed capital was highest in Western Kazakhstan (77%), and then in Mangistau (central Kazakhstan, 66%), East Kazakhstan (57%), Almaty (56%) and Aktubinsk (western Kazakhstan, 48%).

Basic Parameters for the Construction Industry's Long-term Development Strategy

The construction industry provides a favorable investment climate for foreign investors. There are 153 joint ventures with foreign firms and 102 enterprises with 100% foreign capital (operating as affiliates). Most of the main industrial enterprises in this sector have been transferred into foreign management. The Karaganda cement factory was transferred to the foreign company Central Asia Cement (Malaysia) and Shymkent Cement JSC was transferred to the management of French companies.

Construction materials and resources. According to several Kazakhstani construction firms, today's market is more results-oriented and time-sensitive, and largely rejects low-quality materials and workmanship. Stock is also a key element for companies because clients want timely delivery of building materials and services. Maintaining inventory poses a financial challenge (and risk) for construction firms operating in Kazakhstan. According to several leading companies, the following construction materials are considered to be in demand: different colored woods for parquet floors and finishing; brick-making equipment; ceramic products (tiles, mats, etc.); plastic builders' ware (including reservoirs, tanks and vats, doors, windows and their frames, door thresholds, shutters, and blinds); carpets and other textile floor coverings; plaster panels; etc.

Many building materials sourced out of Turkey, Dubai, and China are perceived to be of lesser quality. U.S. and European materials enjoy a better reputation for quality and, while more expensive, are preferred by those consumers who are able to pay the higher prices.

Kazakhstani construction companies mainly produce the materials they need themselves, outsourcing raw materials, such as wood and glass, from neighboring countries (mainly from China, Russia, and Kyrgyzstan). They obtain cement, sand, and bricks from local companies. The main cement producers are Vostok Cements, Karaganda Cement, Shymkent Cement, and Semey Cement. The main brick producers are the Almaty Brick and Shymkent Brick plants, although any large center in the country has its own local brick-producing plant.

Operations and logistics. The industry's current manufacturing objective is to improve the standards for delivering materials and resources. The strategy is to keep pace with trends in the construction industry by steadily enhancing quality requirements and standards, while increasing efficiency and lowering costs of materials. Currently, with manufacturing facilities vulnerable to natural disasters and a reduction of resources from suppliers, there has been an increase in the number of local suppliers. This growth is supported by the government. The increasing number of local suppliers creates a trend toward the appropriate mix of people and machines in manufacturing firms. Because of inventory requirements, there is a financial risk for construction firms operating in Kazakhstan. As a result of the analysis of operations and logistics in the construction industry we can say that the operations managers are using appropriate concepts and techniques to evaluate and improve performance. However, this area requires stronger government support for increasing efficiency throughout the industry.

Human resource management. The strategy of human resource management (HRM) in the construction industry is the development of highly professional and skilled staff. The objectives of HRM in this industry are the following: to increase skilled staff by 20% by 2007, to increase the employment rate by 0.5% annually, and to provide 100% of local expert staff needs by 2007.

The policy of HRM in the construction industry is the following: to use foreign training programs for senior specialists for professional growth, to improve bonuses and incentive systems, and to implement the use of more high-tech equipment to increase efficiency of performance.

In the early 1990s, 9% of Kazakhstan's work force was employed in construction. An estimated 28.3% of the work force had at least a secondary education at the time of independence in 1991. Economic growth in the first quarter of 2001 promoted improvements in labor market conditions. In the first quarter of 2001, employment was increased by 36.5% in the construction industries compared to the first quarter of 2000. Construction remained less attractive for women (16%). The construction process demands employees with a certain level of education and skills, and the main suppliers of such specialist training are institutes and colleges with construction specialization. The largest institute providing high-level employees for the construction industry is Almaty Institute of Construction and Architecture. Unskilled laborers are hired from former CIS countries and such countries as China and Turkey where labor is cheaper. HRM provides construction companies with a competitive advantage because these companies have incentives to develop their staffs' skills to European standards in order to be more competitive in a highly competitive market.

The HRM factor plays a key role in the construction industry because this industry is highly dynamic in the development of new technologies and construction techniques. Human resource managers use appropriate concepts and techniques to evaluate and improve industry performance. In this regard, Bazis-A successfully uses job analysis programs, performance appraisal systems, up-to-date job descriptions, training and development programs, attitude surveys, job design programs, and autonomous work teams that help effectively manage and use the company's human resources.

There is no labor union within Bazis-A. Equal opportunity rights are provided to all job applicants. There is no race, sex, or age discrimination in the company when processing applicants. Despite the absence of a labor union, all the rights of employees are satisfied according to national labor laws.

Information systems. The construction industry's information system objectives are to improve efficiency, productivity, quality control, and standardization. The strategy is to gradually implement information technology (IT) systems and techniques within the industry. The objectives and strategy, however, are not clearly stated and there are no established programs and policies. As a consequence, they are not consistent with the industry's mission, objectives, and strategies, and with the internal and external environments.

The construction industry has made significant strides in incorporating information technology into design, detailing, fabrication, erection, and project management. Nevertheless, the industry's information systems are not performing well in terms of providing useful databases, and offering Internet access and Web sites. Funding in this area is insufficient to ensure the strategic advantage and survival of the industry.

The need for updating technologies in the construction industry, increased local and international competition, and the need to improve the profitability of the industry have resulted in IT becoming a major focus in construction. There is a special program for improving information system technologies, but it is not clearly stated, due to insufficient investments in this sector.

The concept of project modeling, or electronic prototyping, is seen by many of the more innovative construction professionals as the only way to improve the record of the industry. In Kazakhstan, construction industry processes have many similarities with manufacturing, with one crucial difference. Corresponding to the manufacturing prototype stage where problems are identified and resolved is, in the construction industry, the finished building. If the information on the contract drawings is incomplete or inaccurate, then the building cannot be built either in the computer or in the field; it is just cheaper by several orders of magnitude to put things right in the computer.

The key to the development of sophisticated software in the construction industry has been computer integration standards. Computer integration standards are a set of formal computing specifications that allow software vendors to make their engineering applications mutually compatible. They are applicable to any software that involves the creation or use of engineering information. The Cimsteel (Computer integrated manufacturing of constructional work) integration standards were specifically designed for steel-framed buildings or similar structures.

Business Strategy Alternatives in the Construction Industry

As the construction industry in Kazakhstan is in a growth stage, there is huge potential for the development of construction organizations in the market. The industry can be divided into three main segments, using the production profiles of the companies: civil construction companies, industrial state-owned construction companies, and specialized construction companies (also owned by the state).

Differentiation strategy. The differentiation strategy is most suitable for civil construction companies due to the latest trends in the internal and external environments. These companies serve the private customer segment where customers require a more sophisticated product mix. High levels of competition inside the segment shrink a company's market share, so a competitive differentiation advantage is critical for such companies in determining and occupying a market niche. With development of the economy, income per capita has risen, and customers have more bargaining power than before. In comparison to the past, the range of customer needs, preferences, and expectations has grown. For these reasons, many private companies are creating brand awareness among their customers and prospective customers.

Focus strategy. Many privately-owned companies have relatively low volume (in comparison with state-owned firms). This means that these companies can serve small segments of customers with differentiated preferences and needs. Large state-owned industrial construction companies, on the other hand, must follow a cost leadership strategy. Price is a critical factor for the customer in this segment. As the customers are mostly governmental bodies and the country's budget often lacks funds, the price of the order is one of the most important factors. Moreover, as these companies experience extremely large volume due to the great capacities they possess and the frequency of large orders (in terms of revenue), such a strategy will provide these companies an opportunity to benefit from economies of scale. As the competition inside the segment is quite developed and most customers are most sensitive to price, there is no need for product differentiation. Customers of this segment are not interested in product mix design, but in price. The market can be identified as limited, because most orders are from the government.

The focus strategy is, therefore, appropriate for the state-owned specialized construction companies, which are the inheritance of the former Soviet Union (military, irrigation, and hydroelectric station construction). This segment is characterized by an extremely low level of competition. There is no chance for them to specialize in their production technologies due to the extremely heavy asset base. The only possible alternative is to sharpen the focus of their production profile. Their production profile includes these factors: they are state owned; they have focused labor force skills; there is no competition; and they have no production facilities for performing varied construction projects.

Business Strategy Alternatives for Bazis-A Corporation

The construction industry in Kazakhstan is booming, and one company that stands out from the competition is Bazis-A Corporation. With its ability to carry out turnkey projects unique in architectural style and technical complexity, it increased its volume from $2 million in 1991 to $80 million in 2002. Bazis-A Corporation has developed its portfolio from constructing standard large-panel multi-story houses and small office buildings, to erecting specially designed buildings utilizing the newest building technologies and materials. It has designed and constructed embassies, banks, buildings for foreign companies, and exclusive apartment complexes.

The main customer of the Bazis-A Corporation is the government. Bazis-A constructed the House of Ministries Building. Their 36-story Ministry of Transport and Communications in Astana was the first skyscraper in the new capital. In addition, Bazis-A Corporation constructs the main buildings for the biggest oil and gas companies of the republic: KazMunaiGas, Oil and Gas Transport, KazTransGas, KazakhOil, KazTransOil, Munai Impex, KazakhOil Service, and Kazakh Oil Products.

The major principles and priorities of the company are connected with civil construction. It always strives to be involved in projects that are strategically essential for the development of Kazakhstan and for the growth of the company. The company's management believes that the economic situation in Kazakhstan requires enterprises to develop precise goals and clear-cut priorities in order to compete on both a local and a global scale for the growth of national wealth, and to possess the ability to realize these goals and priorities.

These are the goals and principles of Bazis-A: to develop the civil construction sector, to create favorable conditions for investors, to co-operate long-term with investors based on parity, and to comply strictly with all agreements and contracts. Regarding the implementation of new projects and the diversification of its activities, Bazis-A aims to coordinate and consolidate its joint ventures into a single system.

Taking into account the marketing trends inside the civil construction sector of the industry (increased number of households, upper and upper-middle social classes) as well as external factors (growth of GDP and average income per capita), the most appropriate and beneficial business strategy for Bazis-A is product differentiation. Competitive advantage is vital for Bazis-A, so the company is positioning its products as unique and of high quality. The company needs to deal with a wide range of customer needs, preferences, and expectations, and is in the process of creating brand awareness among its customers. Bazis-A has relatively low volume in this segment (in comparison with other state-owned enterprises), and has a trained and educated labor force. Bazis-A has the required production facilities and techniques, and its level of brand recognition is quite good. (Caveat: despite the reasons for pursuing this strategy, however, it might negatively affect the business by increasing expenses, shrinking the customer base, and overtaxing their capacity.)

Chapter 8

The Food Industry: Old and New Ways Coexist in Kazakhstan

Introduction

The nomadic life of the Central Asian *steppe* has adapted to the terrain and climate for centuries; the basic necessities of life (food, shelter, and clothing), what they eat, what they wear, and where they live, have not changed. This has been the case during the times of Tsars and during the occupation by the Soviet Union. What has changed since independence is the availability of imported food items in local department stores. Kazakhstanis generally eat meat, poultry, and vegetable products. Historically, families moved from place to place, taking with them sheep, horses, and other animals, for grazing and herding of their flocks. The modern Kazakhstan has, to some extent, disrupted the nomadic life of the past; with modern transportation, roads, and oil revenues, the republic has witnessed the modernization of food delivery and distribution.

It is not common for consumers in the food industry to make their purchasing decisions based on their preferences in product name, brand, or, packaging. For example, in spite of the fact that "Seimar" is a well-known brand of eggs, a customer will not go to another shop to find exactly this brand if there are eggs "without a brand name," and would buy them even if they are straight from a farm. Packaging represents an important aspect when making purchasing decisions, yet, it is not critical for the customer.

In general, meat and fruits may cost the same throughout the country, with small differences in prices across the republic. However, many other food products are still imported into Kazakhstan (mostly from Russia), which gives local producers a price advantage. In addition to pricing policies, the availability of food products is another important factor; for instance, milk bought from old ladies, called "pensioners," who sell from their farms in plastic bottles, is cheaper than milk purchased from corner (neighborhood) shops. Once again, the consumers do not show any special preference to the milk products sold in the shops (including packaging and hygiene factors); so both types of purchases are considered competitive.

Changing consumer preferences is one of the driving forces behind changing food selections and, in turn, demand for marketing services needed to transform food stuffs from raw agricultural commodities to packaged retail food products. The growing economy since independence has raised incomes and allowed consumers to pay for convenience. Also, in major cities, two-income families have limited time for preparing food at home, thereby raising the demand for fast and convenient shops. The farm-to-retail price spread measures the contributions of food producers, wholesalers, and retail firms. Recent increases in consumer demand for convenience have increased the need for marketing services provided by department and other retail stores, which of course increases the overall price spread and the food industry's marketing costs.

Industry Overview

The food processing industry plays an important role in Kazakhstan's economic development. Its dominance is by almost a third of the industrial production (36.4% in 1991; 34.9% in 2001 and 37.1% in 2002). In recent years the food processing industry in Kazakhstan has made relatively stable progress. The food industry is developing dynamically and also is very attractive for investments and entrepreneurship. In 1991 the number of companies producing food products was 26 times less than in year 2001 (12 companies in 1991, 287 companies in 2001 and 313 in

2002). Most of these companies (86.3%) are small enterprises with less than 50 employees and the rest are medium and big ones. Almost 36% of all companies produce "other products" which include bread, baking products, confectionary, spaghetti, mayonnaise, tea, ketchup, and mustard; around 33% produce beverages; 0.3% produce fodder; 5.7% produce flour and starch; 3.9% produce dairy products; 8.6% produce vegetable oil and animal fat; 8% produce processed and preserved fruits and vegetables; 0.15% produce processed and preserved fish; and 4.7% produce meat and meat products. (A typical breakdown of the volume of the food production is shown in Figure 8-1.)

Food industry goals are to: promote an environment leading to increased competitiveness; promote increased consumption of Kazakhstan

Figure 8-1
Breakdown of Food Production Industry by Category, 2002

Meat	4.7%
Processed and preserved fruits and vegetables	8.0%
Vegetable oil and animal fat	8.6%
Milk foods	3.9%
Flour and cereal foods	5.7%
Finished fodders	0.3%
Beverage	33.0%
Processed and preserved fish	0.15%
Others	36.0%

Source: National Statistics Agency of Kazakhstan

food industry products; promote export market development; promote the development of food safety programs which provide sustained confidence in the safety of products sold to Kazakhstan consumers; promote the adoption of legislation / policies that fairly balance stakeholder interests within the Kazakhstan food industry; promote legislation and policy development consistent with the goals of the food industry to achieve predictability, sustainability and a level playing field regarding legislative and regulatory matters of domestic food production; increase the number of jobs in the food industry; develop food industry technologies and methods both to improve production and safeguard the environment, emphasizing where possible those technologies that employ pollution prevention rather than pollution control techniques; and finally, increase exports of Kazakhstani food products.

Industry Governance

It appears there is no direct ministry or state body that could regulate all operations of the food industry. Each ministry is obligated to regulate relations within the food industry in its own limited response, in terms of direct concern. This is positive because it provides a framework for checks and balances from all sides of regulation and control, and by each state institution. On the one hand, it could be considered as an advantage but, on the other hand, it could be considered as a disadvantage. Most close to the food industry are the Ministry of Industry and Trade and the Ministry of Agriculture. The internal structures of each ministry often change and are reorganized.

External Environment

The figure on the facing page represents what general environmental forces are currently affecting the food industry in Kazakhstan (this is commonly referred to as PEST [political, economic, socio-cultural, and technical] analysis).

The Task Environment (Porter's Model) in the Food Industry

Barriers to entry: The food industry is characterized by comparatively low barriers to entry. Indicative of this are the product's production features. Is it a locally produced or imported product; were the raw materials supplied by local companies or private persons, or were they imported? The market consists of big companies, small enterprises, private persons, and import

Figure 8-2
PEST Analysis

Political-legal	Economic
• Government programs supporting food industry • Laws setting new embargoes or tariffs • New taxation policy • Rapid growth of oil & gas sector • Comparatively low tariffs on imported goods	• Inflation rate • New investors • Bank credit policy • Fluctuating tenge on the world exchange market • Entrance of new foreign food manufacturers • Increase or decrease in people's income • Economic crisis
Socio-cultural	**Technological**
• Move of preferences to buy only foreign food or to buy only domestic food • Distrust of foreign food manufacturers or distrust of domestic ones • High level of loyalty to domestically produced products	• New methods of manufacturing • New technology, equipment • Use of old technologies

firms. Taking into account the rapid growth of the food industry, it is possible to say that new companies could easily enter into the market and operate there with clearly defined strategies and objectives. Local companies and enterprises, in terms of imported products like bakeries, confectioneries, citrus fruits, and others could face the highest barriers to entry because of several factors impossible to produce domestically. Local producers are mostly vertically integrated which causes a decrease in the suppliers' power and the cost of manufacturing. Another important part is the growing loyalty of customers to the locally produced product. Due to these conditions of the market, entry is positive, and does not create strong obstacles.

Rivalry Degree: Competition in the food industry becomes stronger between local producers and import firms. Customer preferences play the main determinate role in buying preferences. However, in each type of product produced, there are few companies that compete. But the soft drink market is a bit different. There is strong competition between local producers, and also from foreign firms. In order to stabilize the positions of some domestic companies and to enter the international market, they have had to consolidate with each other. Three of the leading local Kazakhstani companies, RG Brands (juice producer), PRG Bottlers (exclusive producers of "Pepsi" in Kazakhstan), and Tea Land (a tea company) have united in one giant enterprise, RG Brands JSC, to become one of the biggest companies in Central Asia, with a future orientation towards world markets. The consolidated company's strategic partner is Uni Commerce Ltd—official distributor of Nestle, Johnson & Johnson, Unilever and other multi-national companies.

The bargaining power of suppliers is not strong because of the availability of raw materials due to the positive climate conditions that allow the growing of many kinds of vegetables, fruits, crops and other materials. The vertical integration of firms means that the companies themselves grow the necessary materials (like crops, cows, fruits for juices) to produce the finished goods, with low tariffs for imported materials from Uzbekistan, and the nearest courtiers. Big companies like Bekker, which produces beef sausages, have their own cow farmers, or import some ingredients for beer production.

In the last few years consumer supply has been very high. To achieve goals, local companies need to grow faster than the market does. This takes the maximum mobility of all firms' resources, fast reaction to any changes, and professional management. For example, in 2006, when the juice market grew by more than 35% in comparison with 2005, the sales increased by 40%. And when the beverage market went up by 7%, the sales grew by 50%.

The bargaining power of customers is high due to the wide range of products offered by the local and import producers. Consumers could easily switch from one product to another, and receive products with similar high quality and level of service. Obviously it is the impact of rapid industry growth, and the ability of producers to achieve their direct goals.

Substitutes: Food industry products may be easily substituted; this is due to the high degree of rivalry between products offered, cultural features, climate conditions, and people-oriented ways. For example, butter could be substituted by margarine, sausages by meat, café by tea, etc.

SWOT (Strengths, Weaknesses, Opportunities, Threats) Analysis of Food Industry:

Strengths: The rapid growth of the whole industry; a full line of products; comparatively low prices; the vertical integration of companies; the increasing loyalty of customers to domestically produced goods; a high level of quality; a clean and green production environment; and strongly committed industry participants with diverse skills.

Threats: The unstable political situation in the world that affects the Kazakhstan economic environment; future decreased oil prices; the lack of species-specific safety data, fact sheets and standards acceptable to end-users and regulators; the lack of promotion and training (from grower through consumer); and inappropriate price structures.

Weaknesses: The lack of an integrated IT system; fragmentation and lack of collaboration within the industry; generic market information is scarce or lacking; potential imbalances between supply and demand; a lack of substantial existing markets; variations in product supply and quality; comprehensive agronomic information is unavailable; the lack of information on and understanding of food safety issues (safety, product handling and food preparation); and the research base is very small.

Opportunities: To exploit areas where food is not currently produced and establish new cropping industries; to combine cropping with environmental remediation and conservation; to search for, create and exploit new markets at home and abroad; to use the expertise of the established food industry in adding value to native foods; and to interact positively with and strengthen other industries.

Food Industry Structure: The closest to the food industry are the Ministry of Industry and Trade, and the Ministry of Agriculture. The internal structures of each ministry often change and are reorganized. The current structure of the ministries is clear: each consists of a head of the ministry, who has four vice-ministers, one of whom is the first vice-minister. The two ministers who most directly regulate the relations of the food industry are the Minister of Industry and the Minister of Agriculture.

Industry Culture: The food-processing industry of Kazakhstan, after the deep recession of the last few years, has increased its volume of production. In this branch, the updating of a fixed capital, developments of new kinds of production, and quality improvement have taken place. However, positive tendencies in the field are connected to manufacturers that are not mostly oriented towards the processing of agricultural raw materials. They are, first of all, oriented towards the manufacture of alcoholic beverages and fruit drinks, beer, tea, and sunflower oils.

The amount of production has grown (from 1994 to 1997) from 33.783 to 137.653 million tenge while there has been a simultaneous reduction in the number of industrial staff (from 138 to 92 thousand people). Profit levels fluctuated between 3067 and 3897 million tenge, although the overall level of profitability reduced from 14.2% in 1994 to 6.2% in 1997. However, in recent years, especially since 2005, both profits and workforce size have steadily grown. The food industry is highly government regulated through different organizations, which control standards and compliance of the companies. There are many organizations, such as sanitary and epidemiological institutions, and the department of product standardization that are part of this process. The food industry employees are required to have special skills, and are continuously trained in order to produce high quality product.

Food Industry Resources (Marketing, Export/Import)

Food marketing today has become more consumer-oriented and competitive. Changing lifestyles and incomes; growing awareness of health issues; concerns over the quality and quantity of foods available;

demands for products lower in sodium, fat, and cholesterol; consumers desiring more convenience and service; cultural factors; and labeling issues have altered the patterns of demand for food consumption and production worldwide.

Exporting to foreign countries requires the ability to respond to consumer needs and desires in the food they buy, identifying and surveying market groups, who respond to products and services offered in the market place, and knowledge of the conditions and customs in the recipient country, such as labeling products in the language of the receiving nation with its domestic measuring system.

Development of the food processing industry in Kazakhstan is a very important priority task for the development of the agro-industrial sector of the country. This sector has attracted considerable foreign direct investment. At the present time, some changes in consumer behavior may be observed. There are a number of international trends, which continue to drive how we must present our products for sale. The two factors that are consistent throughout the world are: (1) *Health*: Healthy eating is at the forefront of the customers' demands, and we must develop systems that clearly show that on the labels. It does not have to be organic, but produce that has been raised under free-range farming methods has an advantage. (2) *Convenience*: Convenience is a must. We know that the customers we are targeting have: a high income bracket; long working hours; and limited shopping time. They require that: products be prepared and ready within 20 minutes; products are fresh; and packaging size is appropriate for smaller families. They may be cash rich, but they are time poor, and we must therefore tailor our products to meet their demands.

The share of food products in the country's export-import business is quite high. In the last years, the volume of export was 13.9-18.6%, import, 7.6-8.5%. The share of export has increased from 2000 to 2002 at 2.5%, the share of the import, however, decreased by 0.9%. The major kinds of exported products are flour, sugar, vodka, and rice; imports are milk and cream, honey, wines, cheeses. The import substitution program in the light and food industries in 2001-2003 and the agricultural food program in 2003-2005 provided the competitiveness of food and agricultural products. In line with the food program, the state plans to increase considerably the financing of the agricultural industry within the next three years. Specifically, the allocations provided by the budget in 2003 compared to 2001 have increased by 9.9 billion Tenge. Kazakhstan will continue to pursue development of the food industry in the coming years. It is to be noted that the marketing objectives, policies and programs still are determined mostly by government and budget regulations.

The food industry, as was mentioned before, plays an important role in the economy. The market offers to consumers both domestically produced products, and also products from international companies. There are more world-recognized companies than ever before coming to the market of the Republic of Kazakhstan to offer ingredients and food additives. This speaks for the development of the food industry in the republic.

The wave of imported food products responds to the growing demands of Kazakhstan consumers. This caters big opportunities to foreign producers and suppliers. Currently, the food ingredients market in Kazakhstan is characterized by imports. A surge of imported food products is meeting the growing demand of Kazakhstan consumers, especially for candies, cakes, potato chips, etc. This presents opportunities for international firms. Companies active in this sector are usually big multi-nationals who are able to work through their European-based branches.

The food industry is one of the priority sectors in the processing industry. According to official statistics, there are more new shops being opened and finished products plants being constructed in the industry. The main tasks in industrial production are to develop local labor-intensive industries and facilities oriented towards the home consumers' market. At the moment, the country has almost 16,000 operating enterprises of which 1.6% (nearly 250 large enterprises) produces more than 77% of all Kazakhstan food products.

New trends and marketing ideas are often introduced early within the food sector. It includes some of the biggest and most internationalized consumer product companies. The product life cycle is especially short for food products, which calls for innovation and a constant development of new products and marketing ideas. Furthermore, food products involve specific logistical requirements. Consumers are also particularly sensitive to the quality and the characteristics of food products because they directly influence health and well being.

Distribution in the Food Industry

In general, there are two possible schemes of distribution in the food industry:

```
                                      - Specialized shops
                                      - Bazaars (market)
1. Manufacturer ──► Wholesaler ──►    - Kiosks
   Selling           Distributor      - "Babushkas" (persons standing alone
                                        selling on the streets)
                                      - Public places (restaurants, cafes,
                                        hospitals)
                                      - Supermarkets
```

```
2. Manufacturer ──► Own shop (manufacturers)
                    Public places (restaurants, cafes, organizations, hospitals)
```

The most popular types of product promotion of food manufacturers are: 1. Outdoor and TV advertising; 2. Trade shows. Outdoor advertising includes billboards (usually at bus-stops), small sheets throughout the cities, etc. TV advertising is popular by bigger players in the industry—those who promote the brand mostly (Seimar, Food master, Sultan). Trade shows have gained popularity because they make it possible to represent products to all parties involved—wholesalers, distributors, food industry manufacturers, representatives of commercial organizations, supermarkets, etc. The main objectives of such trade shows are to attract new companies and investments and to develop international and internal economic relations.

Usually, such trade shows are supported by the Ministry of Agriculture of the Republic of Kazakhstan, and/or the Ministry of Economic Development and Trade of the Republic of Kazakhstan. Other promotional means used in the food industry are: "Point-of-sale" advertising (posters, brochures, plastic bags with company's logo, slogan, and/or products)—at the places where the products are sold (shops); Trade advertising—ads in food publications to encourage users to check out new products and the added benefits. Trade publicity—companies continually publish messages in the magazines and newspapers read by both intermediary and final customers.

Industry Profitability

In 1999 and 2000, food manufacturers had negative results in operation, but it is necessary to mention that the losses had a decreasing trend and subsequently the food industry became profitable. A positive balance of incomes and losses of medium and large businesses formed annually; meanwhile most small businesses had losses (See **Figure 8-5**).

In the analyzed period, a positive balance of incomes and losses was only in meat production, production of vegetable oil and animal fat, and beverage production. The manufacturers of finished fodders for domestic animals had losses as shown in **Figure 8-4**.

The share of unprofitable food-stuffs manufacturers increased from year to year in comparison with the manufacturing industry and average in Almaty. The highest share of unprofitable businesses was in production of meat, finished fodders for domestic animals and other food-stuffs as seen from **Figure 8-6**.

The share of unprofitable food manufacturers in small businesses was higher than the share of unprofitable manufacturers in medium and large businesses in both the manufacturing industry and as a whole in Almaty. The main reasons for this are less competitiveness of small businesses and greater risks in the attempts to capture the market.

The high level share of unprofitable food manufacturers has a negative impact on the indicators of the whole food industry. In the analyzed period, profitability of the food-stuffs manufacturers was lower than in the

Table 8-3
Food Industry Sales, in millions of Tenge

| | 1999 | 2000 | 2001 | 2002 | | |
				Quarter I	Quarter II	Quarter III
Food-stuffs production:	19,573.80	27,022.20	38,362.30	9,504.5	11,884.10	12,187.90
Meat	925.00	1,353.40	1,720.00	410.60	456.80	480.70
Processed and preserved fish	71.40	72.70	81.70	25.40	22.40	25.70
Processed and preserved fruits and vegetables	155.00	665.30	1,091.90	355.10	288.50	276.60
Vegetable oil and animal fat	1,223.70	1,763.60	5,496.10	1,388.80	1,420.70	1,356.40
Milk foods	757.60	744.40	787.40	429.80	493.60	473.90
Flour and cereal foods	1,429.20	1,719.80	2,507.80	445.00	492.00	638.30
Beverages	7,149.40	10,076.50	13,984.50	3,215.20	4,565.40	4,987.70
Finished fodders		158.50	160.30	25.30	7.20	4.90
Others	7,862.50	10,468.00	2,532.60	3,209.30	4,137.50	3,943.70

Source: National Statistics Agency of Kazakhstan

manufacturing industry and average in Almaty. It can be visually seen on Figure 8-7.

Meat manufacturers had the highest profitability in the industry; and manufacturers of finished fodders and processed and preserved fruits and vegetables had the lowest profitableness or even losses (See Figure 8-8).

It is necessary to mention that the expenditures of food manufacturers

Figure 8-4
Profit (*Loss*), mln tenge

	1999	2000	2001	2002		
				1st quarter	2nd quarter	3rd quarter
Food-stuffs production	-4,503.70	-447.60	1,977.20	149.60	77.10	311.30
Meat	148.10	99.30	73.30	24.10	22.40	33.80
Processed and preserved fish	-0.40	-0.80	0.90	0.50	-0.70	1.70
Processed and preserved fruits and vegetables	-243.80	-47.70	20.00	-91.90	-37.60	-31.50
Vegetable oil and animal fat	-1031.00	-428.70	359.90	72.40	65.20	55.80
Milk foods	30.10	27.50	-8.30	-10.30	-61.00	-29.40
Flour and cereal foods	-169.10	-129.10	76.30	-7.40	-57.80	-78.00
Beverages	-3,488.80	-115.20	1209.90	57.30	38.10	350.80
Finished fodders	--	-4.50	-11.20	-4.80	-2.80	-4.00
Others	251.20	151.60	256.40	109.70	111.30	12.10

Source: National Statistics Agency of Kazakhstan

Figure 8-5
Cash Flow of Food Production Businesses
(in million tenge)

	1999	2000	2001	2002		
				1st quarter	2nd quarter	3rd quarter
Small businesses	-1488.5	-509.3	-716.1	-124.6	-140.5	-193.6
Medium and large businesses	-3015.2	61.7	1261.1	274.3	217.6	504.9
Total	-4503.7	-447.6	545.0	149.7	77.1	311.3

Source: National Statistics Agency of Kazakhstan

Figure 8-6
Percent of Food Manufacturing Companies Experiencing Loss
(by Sector)

	1999	2000	2001	2002		
				1st quarter	2nd quarter	3rd quarter
Food-stuffs production	51.80	45.70	43.90	37.60	41.80	39.30
Meat	53.80	40.00	44.80	44.40	44.00	24.10
Processed and preserved fish	50.00	33.30	27.30	20.00	36.40	33.30
Processed and preserved fruits and vegetables	100.00	20.00	16.70	33.30	33.30	50.00
Vegetable oil and animal fat	33.30	40.00		14.30		14.30
Milk foods	50.00	50.00	46.70	43.80	50.00	45.80
Flour and cereal foods	36.40	39.40	43.60	42.20	51.20	38.10
Beverages	51.90	42.20	47.40	49.10	33.30	41.90
Finished fodders	--	100.00	60.00	100.00	50.00	50.00
Others	56.50	51.90	46.20	29.20	44.00	41.60

Source: National Statistics Agency of Kazakhstan

Figure 8-7
% Change in Food Manufacturers' Profitability

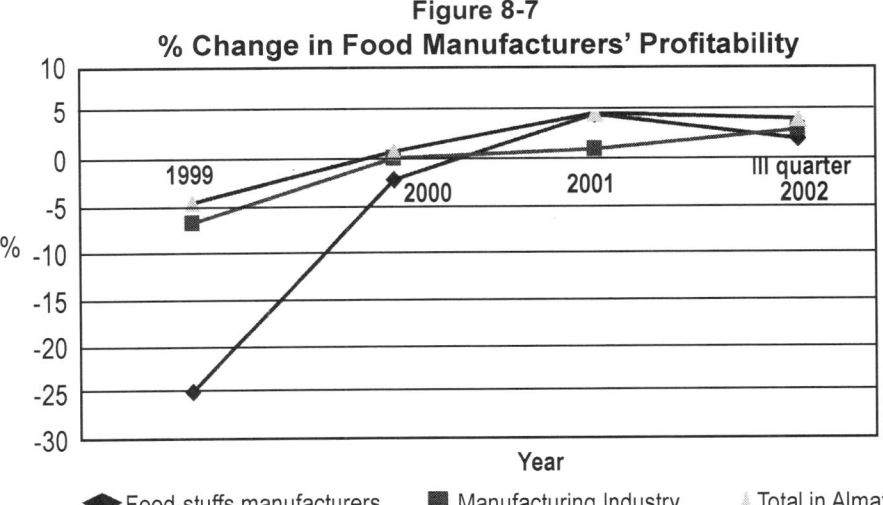

Figure 8-8
Profitability of Food Manufacturers
(% change)

	1999	2000	2001	2002		
				1st quarter	2nd quarter	3rd quarter
Food-stuffs production	-23.60	-1.60	5.30	1.60	0.70	2.70
Meat	19.00	7.80	4.40	6.10	5.10	7.50
Processed and preserved fish	-0.50	-1.10	1.10	1.90	-2.90	7.30
Processed and preserved fruits and vegetables	-18.60	-6.60	1.80	-28.20	-13.90	-11.50
Vegetable oil and animal fat	-45.70	-20.10	6.90	5.60	4.90	4.30
Milk foods	4.10	3.80	-1.00	-2.30	-11.40	-6.20
Flour and cereal foods	-11.70	-7.10	3.20	-1.60	-10.50	-10.80
Beverages	-55.40	-1.20	8.90	1.80	0.90	7.80
Finished fodders	--	-2.80	-6.50	-16.20	-10.60	-12.00
Others	3.40	1.50	2.10	3.50	2.70	0.30

Source: National Statistics Agency of Kazakhstan

increased constantly. In the cost structure, the highest share of expenses belongs to raw materials and other expenses that are connected with general and administration activity. These are shown in Table 8-9.

There were changes in the cost structure during the last years. The observed increase was in the share of raw materials and there was a decrease in the share of direct labor. The food industry is a raw material-intensive industry. In 2000, per unit consumption of material was 0.78 tenge when in 2000, it was 0.76 tenge.

Figure 8-9
Breakdown of food industry expenses as percent of all expenses

	1999	2000	2001	9 months 2002
Raw material	42.9	58.3	62.8	59.1
Direct labor	17.1	7.3	6.1	4.7
Depreciation	10.5	3.9	3.8	7.5
Other expenses	29.5	30.5	27.3	28.7
Total	100.0	100.0	100.0	100.0

Source: National Statistics Agency of Kazakhstan

Industry Liquidity

At the end of the third quarter of 2002, the accounts receivable of food manufacturers were 11026.7 mln tenge (2.3% from city volume) that is by comparison 38.3% more than in the beginning of 2002. Small businesses had 30.8% of total receivables, medium and large ones–9.2%. The major part of receivables is formed by receivables for goods and service, which is 40% of the total. The manufacturers of beverages (44.6%), flour and cereal (14.2%), and vegetable oil and animal fat (11.1%) had the largest receivables in the industry.

As concerning debts, they were 32249.4 mln tenge at the end of the third quarter of 2002, that is 20.0% more as compared with the beginning of 2002. The medium and large businesses had 77.1% of total debts, when small ones had 22.9%. The largest part of debts (80%) belongs to payables to suppliers and contractors and also bank loans (Figure 8-10): manufacturers of beverages (47.8%), vegetable oil and animal fat (16.2%) and flour and cereals also had the highest debts in the industry.

Increases in debts give the manufacturers the opportunity to increase production, use new technology and meet customers' needs. So, "Rahat" offered wider assortments of sweets; "Maslodel" began mayonnaise production; beverage manufacturers, in particular "PRG Bottlers," "Coca-Cola Almaty Bottlers," and "Asem-ai," settled production of non-alcoholic

Figure 8-10
Debt Structure of the Food Production Industry, 2002

Suppliers and contractors	28.4%
Bank Loans	54.3%
Other Payables	17.3%

Source: National Statistics Agency of Kazakhstan

beverages, etc. Share of overdue receivables and payables non-payment were 1.3% and 1.9% correspondingly. Beverage manufacturers had the highest share of receivables and payables–19.6% and 60.3%. At the end of the third quarter of 2002 payables were greater than receivables by 2.9 times when in 2001 this ratio was 3.3. City ratios in this period were 2.1 and 2.4 correspondingly. This fact said that the manufacturers in the food industry had low solvency. At the end of 2001, total assets of the food industry were 40352 mln tenge (or 3.7% of city volume), 46.9% of which were fixed assets and 53.1% were current assets. During 9 months of 2002, total assets increased up to 45320 mln tenge or by 12.3%. At the end of 2001, receivables formed 36.1% of total current assets, inventory 35.0% and cash 14.0%. In the structure of funds source equity was 13483 mln tenge or 33.4% and liabilities were 26885 mln tenge or 66.6%. Debt-to-equity ratio was 0.5 against 0.25 as a whole in Almaty. Assets-to-equity ratio was 0.71.

Industry Investments

It is common for food manufacturers to invest in the acquisition of fixed assets. So, in 2001 investments in fixed assets were 5833.6 mln tenge and at the end of the third quarter of 2002 they were 2187.4 mln tenge. In the food industry, beverage manufacturers and flour and cereal manufacturers make the largest investments in assets (See Table 8-12).

Development of the food industry has a progressive way. There is a constant growth of production volume and share of food product in the total volume of industry production. Equipment and technology are more modernized as a result of investments. But on the other hand, most food manufacturers have problems with losses and a great amount of liabilities. There are opportunities for better capacity utilization, inventory reduction, and closer integration with suppliers of food at various levels. Equally there is the potential of gaining a value advantage in the marketplace through superior customer service. The policy of food industry logistics behind the logistics concept is that of planning and coordinating the materials flow source to the user as an integrated system rather than, as was so often the case in the past, managing the flow as a series of independent activities.

Figure 8-11
Gaining the Competitive Advantage through Logistics

Value advantage
Logistics leverage opportunities
➤ Tailored services
➤ Reliability
➤ Responsiveness

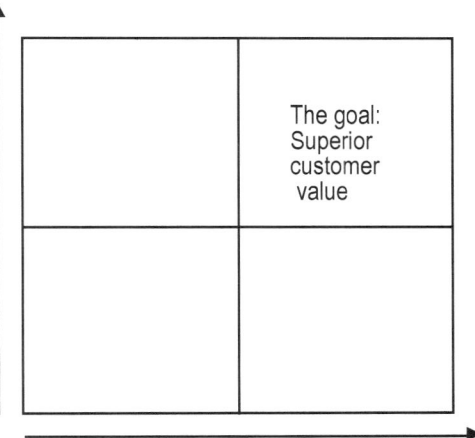

Productivity advantage
Logistics leverage opportunities

➤ Capacity utilization
➤ Asset turn
➤ Co-makers/ schedule integration etc.

Thus, under the logistics management regime of this highly competitive food industry, the goal is to link the marketplace, the distribution network, the manufacturing process and the procurement activity in such a way that customers are serviced at higher levels and yet at lower cost.

The supply chain is the network of organizations that are involved, through upstream and downstream linkages, in the different processes and activities that produce value, in the form of products and services, in the hands of the ultimate consumer. To increase continuously the

Figure 8-12
Investments in Fixed Assets

	2001		9 months 2002	
	mln tenge	%	mln tenge	%
Food-stuffs production:	**5,833.6**	**100.0**	**2,187.4**	**100.0**
Meat	186.8	3.2	72.6	3.3
Processed and preserved fish			0.1	
Processed and preserved fruits and vegetables	36.3	0.6	13.4	0.6
Vegetable oil and animal fat	199.9	3.4	34.7	1.6
Milk foods	200.7	3.4	451.7	20.7
Flour and cereal foods	1,508.7	25.9	188.4	8.6
Beverages	2,841.2	48.7	970.5	44.4
Finished fodders	162.2	2.8	4.7	0.2
Others	697.8	12.0	451.3	20.6

Source: National Statistics Agency of Kazakhstan

number of Kazakhstani companies that understand and realize that the real competition is not company against company, but rather one supply chain against another, is a goal of the food industry.

The number of employees who worked during January-September 2002 was 12,509 or 17.9% of personnel employed in Almaty in manufacturing and 2% out of all employees in the other sectors.

Information System

The information system (IS) today in Kazakhstan represents a slowly developing sector which affects many aspects of the country's life. There is a lack of an integrated information system. Objectives, strategies, and

Figure 8-13
Average Monthly Wage in the Food Industry
(tenge)

	1999	2000	2001	2002		
				1st quarter	2nd quarter	3rd quarter
Small companies	7,908	8,009	9,328	10,820	12,262	13,289
Medium & Large Companies	16,711	18,994	21,807	22,299	23,189	23,441
Average monthly food industry wage as percent of average national wage						
Small	75.7	56.0	51.4	55.5	57.0	59.3
Medium & Large	108.9	102.4	93.2	86.5	84.2	83.8

Source: National Statistics Agency of Kazakhstan

policies of IS are clearly defined but performance and introduction of them are still deficient, which makes a huge impact on the operation activity of the food market players, and the communication tools between them. IS resource is not inconsistent with the food industry objectives, policies, and strategies at all. Starting a short time ago, only a small amount of huge firms created their own database system offering Internet access and Web sites. Huge manufacturers like Food Master, Bekker, and the hard and soft drink producers provided database systems within their own organi-zations which allow them to perform automated routine clerical operations, assist managers in making routine decisions, and provide them with the necessary information for strategic decision making.

Most of the companies still use communication tools like telephones, faxes and other tools that limit opportunities of effective operation activity. They are small companies whose budget is limited, which does not allow them to make investments in an IT system. Additionally, not each of the food firms has their own IS manager, or if there is, then appropriate concepts and techniques to evaluate and improve industry performance are not used. But, the market allows training programs, corresponding to IS companies, for help in creating database systems within the companies. However, analyses indicate a positive trend of implementing the use of

IS within the companies specifically for the food industry. Companies began to understand the importance of IS performance, that it provides a competitive advantage, and would positively affect the future performance of the company's management, and operation itself. Comparing this with other sectors of Kazakhstan's economy, it is approximately the same situation. But, as it was mentioned before, there is a positive trend for IS performance.

Chapter 9

Telecommunication:
Where Global Trends Dominate

Introduction

The Republic of Kazakhstan inherited its telecommunication infrastructure from the time she was under the former Soviet Union, which was obviously not quite as it should have been. Just as in other Central Asian countries under Soviet rule, she did not have any access to Western telecommunication technologies, and this has had the Republic in catch-up mode ever since her independence of 1991.

However, Kazakhstan's disadvantage of having been isolated from the rest of the world should be less problematic for the field of telecommunication, because the enormous technological advancement that impacted the entire world happened only in the last two decades or so, which coincides with the independence of the Republic. For the younger people, that change seems more natural and easier to adapt to the change and, with technological assistance from the West and other highly developed countries, Kazakhstan will catch up with the rest of the world. While the country's manufacturing activities are so far behind, its natural resources would afford her to purchase the necessary equipment from elsewhere. So, with the government's wise administration, Kazakhstan can be part of the globalization, as in most any other society, about accepting advancing technology. People in general, and in particular, seem to enjoy using both wired and wireless communication systems, as well as Internet and e-mail.

Kazakhstan is a multi-cultural society and her people seem to have no problem becoming accustomed to the Western way of doing business. And, there is a low population density (5.5 per square kilometer in 2001), as well as many people work at home. Hence, the usage of cell phones is quite common in urban areas. Providing access to telecommunication service to all the population, particularly for those who live in remote regions, would be a challenge for the government.

However, even with Kazakhstan's disadvantage of having been isolated from the rest of the world, now having to catch up with the rest, at least in this field of telecommunication, should be a little easier because the enormous technological advancement in the world in the field of telecommunication took place particularly in the last two decades or so, which coincides with the time of her independence. Therefore, with other advanced societies' assistance, Kazakhstan should be able to adapt to that phenomenon well, especially the young people. However, as her manufacturing activities are nearly non-existent, all the equipment for the telecommunication business must be imported as well, at least for now.

Government Regulation and Policies

The Ministry of Transport and Communications is responsible for regulating the telecommunication business, and the licensing of stations, mobile systems, and value-added services. More exactly, the Committee on Communications and Information of the Ministry is the body which virtually controls every aspect of the industry. It oversees every matter relating to development and planning, operations, and regulations. The committee members are appointed by the ministry in consultation with the Prime Minister and President. One serious problem it seems to have is that the key administrators and officers tend to stay at their positions for a rather short period of time. Naturally, this has a very negative impact on the industry because the Ministry's policies may change, quite abruptly at times, because of it. The reason for this phenomenon is not clear to outsiders.

At any rate, since her independence, the major player in this field is the government-owned Kazakh Telecom, and it has the predominant position in the field. Currently, however, the government's efforts to improve the general situation would encourage other competitors to join in, as will be discussed in the following sections.

Kazakh Telecom

The major player in the telecommunication business in Kazakhstan is Kazakh Telecom, which is 50% government owned, and covers all areas of the business nationwide. Kazakh Telecom has two types of stock ownerships: preferred and non-preferred. Its Board of Directors represents the investment banks, namely, Central Asia Industrial Investment (with 30.1% ownership) and the Bank of New York (with 6.7% ownership), and also preferred stocks (10%) and others (3.2%).

As mentioned above, this is the company that holds the major share of the domestic and international communication business of Kazakhstan ever since she became independent from the Soviet Union, and holds virtually a monopolistic position for local and long distance, as well as mobile telephone service, and data transmission, both domestic and international. It also provides leased lines, Internet, paging, radio and television broadcasting, and directory and emergency services.

Kazakh Telecom has installed 2.2 million lines of switching capacity and, at the end of June 1999, operated 1.6 million subscriber lines. Soon after independence, Kazakh Telecom began a national program to modernize the country's telecommunication system. It provides the following services: voice telephone (local, intercity, and international) accounting for 94% of revenues; telegraph and telex, 2%; and, Internet, the other 2% of revenues, leasing of channels; satellite "KULAN" (for B2B); Business Network (digital telecommunication networks, which provide local, intercity, and international net for B2B); and "Tarton" and "Smart" cards for taxaphones.

Kazakh Telecom is also the owner of the Public Switch Telephony Network (PSTN), which has 31 subsidiaries. Kazakh Telecom controls other sectors of the telecommunications industry and accounts for the high entry barriers facing new companies that want to establish operations in Kazakhstan.

Kazakh Telecom has several subsidiaries and branches: they are, GSM Kazakhstan (51% owned by Kazakh Telecom), a cell network operator (K-cell and K-mobile) in the GSM format; Aftel, a cell network operator (50% owned by Kazakh Telecom); Arna Sprint Data Communications (50% owned by Kazakh Telecom); and Kaznet (100% owned by Kazakh Telecom) telecommunications company; and a large operator, Nursat (41% owned by Kazakh Telecom). The level of Kazakh Telecom's involvement in the operations of the telecommunications industry is significant and no important decision can be made without their participation.

The number of people employed by Kazakh Telecom is much larger than in smaller companies directed toward corporate business with advanced equipment, ISP or the wireless business segment. However, the introduction of modern technologies allowed all telecommunication companies to cut personnel. For example, Kazakh Telecom reduced the number of employees from 50,000 to 31,000 in 2005. Kazakh Telecom was able to increase the effectiveness of their personnel by increasing the number of lines per employee from 59 in 2000 to 85 in 2005. The company's management is reportedly considering cutting personnel further. It is expected that the replacement of analog equipment with digital will let the company save on maintenance and repair expenses. Less labor-intensive equipment installation, automation of production processes, and optimization of the controlling processes will allow the company to cut employees down another 4,000 by the year 2012.

Other Providers of Telecommunication Services

Lucent, which provides international, inter-city, and local networks, is the leader in the Kazakhstani market. It serves the major players of the market such as Kazakh Telecom, Nursat, and Kazakhstan Temir Zholi, and provides Lucent Wireless and network SDH equipment. Germany's

Siemens has participation in the following projects: Trans-Asian-European Line; National Information Super Highway; and telecommunications infrastructure for the Caspian Pipeline Consortium Project. Also Siemens serves many large companies in Kazakhstan: KEGOK, Kazakhstan Temir Zholi; KazAeroNavigation, KazTransOil, etc. The Canadian company, Nortel, operates in Kazakhstan through a Turkish subsidiary. Its factory for production of telecommunication equipment is in Pavlodar. Nortel also provides its equipment through its Kazakhstan office, VesNet. In 2001, an American company and a world leader in the production of network equipment, Cisco System, started providing equipment.

In spite of the lack of competition, there are many large and small companies competing in Kazakhstan's telecommunications industry. Other large foreign competitors, such as Ducat, Nursat, Altel, and TNS Plus, operate in certain sectors of the industry. They have their own lines, equipment, and connections.

Ducat, a provider of a wide range of telecommunication products, not including cellular communications, is Kazakh Telecom's main competitor in serving B2B customers. The company has a 60% market share in serving corporate clients in Almaty. Ducat uses advanced technology and its quality of service corresponds to international standards. Ducat offers the following services: voice telephony; fax service (local and international); Internet access, Web services; global networks; ISDN services, and Ducat NetCard.

Nursat's main customers are corporate clients who need high quality services, IP telephony, transmission of video materials, etc. Nursat's services include telephone networks (local, inter-city, and international); Internet access; VOIP telephony, construction of corporate networks; satellite net; Web design; and delivery of telecommunication equipment.

The telecom industry structure is highly centralized around the major player, Kazakh Telecom, but the other participants do collaborate with the giant. The industry culture is evolving and companies are beginning to develop corporate cultures, teamwork, and education and training programs. Until now, productivity and the quality of performance were concerns of only the competitive private companies, but Kazakh Telecom is now beginning to pay attention to improving its own quality of performance as well.

In the telecommunications market, the bargaining power of consumers remains low (medium in the ISP and Internet sector). Switching costs are high and using an alternate supplier means changing lines or location because of the lack of competition in the industry. Telephone systems remain a key factor for any business in Kazakhstan. Therefore, because of the need for the use of the telephone, businesses will pay almost any price for that service.

Equipment, etc.

As in many other industries, Kazakhstan's manufacturing of wireless telecommunications equipment and supplies is non-existent. Therefore, all equipment and supplies must be imported. The total market share of Western suppliers in 1999 was $4.8 million and is estimated to increase to well over $10 million by 2012. The market share of the newly independent states (NIS) was $474,700, and, that of Russia was $473,500. Most wireless communications equipment is imported from the U.S., Israel, Japan, and Europe. These companies are: RAD Data Communications, Breezecom, GILAT, Ericsson, Siemens, Nokia, EICON Technologies, Philips, Kenwood, Liebert, Icom, Yaesu/Vertex, Codan, Barret, SGC, AirNet, Lucent, Cisco, Nortel, and Alcatel. The primary suppliers of telecommunication equipment were Siemens and Lucent, and they are the suppliers for Kazakh Telecom, large corporations, and government organizations.

Wireless Communications

In 2001 there was phenomenal growth in wireless communication systems in Kazakhstan. The share of cell-phone operators in the tele-communications market increased from 3% to 26%, and the number of users increased more than eight times (from 98,700 in 2000 to 834,500 in 2001). The revenues from this service increased by 207% in 2003 compared to revenues in 2002. The market for cell operators is divided among GSM-Kazakhstan, Kar-Tel, and Altel. The first two work in digital standard; Altel continues to provide service in analog mode, AMPS/NAM PS.

Kar-Tel (trademark, K-Mobile) is a joint venture between the Turkish company Rumeli Telecom and the Kazakhstani company, Investel. GSM-Kazakhstan (trademark, K-Cell) is a joint venture between the Turkish company, Turkcell, and Kazakh Telecom. Altel is a joint venture with the U.S. Metromedia Group. The operators have partnership agreements with Motorola, Ericsson, Nokia, and other equipment suppliers.

GSM-Kazakhstan has a number of advantages: low cost of airtime; free incoming calls; confidentiality; noise immunity; high quality of voice transmission; and international roaming. Turkcell has already invested nearly half a billion dollars to gain a leading position in the development of cellular communications in Kazakhstan. In 2001, K-Cell established a full network for Kazakhstani cities and urban-type villages with populations of 50,000 and more. K-Cell continues to increase subscriber capacity and its share of the market. K-Mobile has a fifteen-year operator license for which the company paid $67.5 million. Its investment during the first three years of operation is estimated to have been $160 million.

For service providers, the cost of telecommunications equipment remains a decisive factor. The user fees of GSM in Kazakhstan are still high in comparison with those in Asia and in Europe. Concerning the current trend in the telecommunications market regarding price policy, the following can be said: for PSTN (Public Switch Telephony Network) services, there is reasonable pricing for local calls, but unreasonably high prices for international calls; for VOIP there are low prices (adequate for the quality, which is extremely low); and for wireless services there are high prices.

Development of a high-capacity national infrastructure, securing rapid introduction of new technologies in all spheres of the economy and management, is an indispensable condition for creation of a uniform information environment and Kazakhstan's integration into the global intelligence infrastructure.

Modernization Process

In 1997, the program for the modernization and development of the PSTN (Public Switch Telephony Network) was designed for the years 1998-2005. The main goals of this program were building the National Information Highway (NIH) based on fiber-optic lines; modernizing and developing local telecommunications networks; building inter-city and intra-zone networks; replacing analogous systems with digital; and developing data transmission networks, corporate networks, and synchronization.

The modernization process includes all levels and components of the national telecommunications network. The following significant modernization projects have renovated and enlarged the network: (1) The TransAsianEuropean (TAE) fiber-optic line (1,750 km) was built in Kazakhstan; the northern fiber-optic line (137 km) was built from Petropavlovsk (Kazakhstan) to Kornilovka (Russia); (2) The western fiber-optic lines of the NIH (2,538 km), connecting Shymkent, Kyzylorda, Atyrau, and Ganyushkino, were built; (3) The digital radio-relay line (1,140 km), from Almaty to Karaganda, was built. This provided a new higher level of quality for digital access to Russia through Almaty, Karaganda, Astana, Kokshetau, and Petropavlovsk; (4) Digital flow of 34 Mbit/s was organized by means of an analog radio-relay line connecting Astana, Ust-Kamenogorsk, and Almaty. This also provided for cellular communication needs to the level of the GSM standard; (5) The reconstruction of the Orbita satellite station was completed in Almaty. International satellite systems, Intelsat, were installed in Almaty, Aktau, and Atyrau, so that channels of satellite connection were organized among them, and connections with Germany, England, Switzerland, Russia, UAE, and Canada were established; (6) Further expansion of the DAMA satellite network, a system of multichannel satellites providing communications in rural and remote areas, was completed. It made 200 channels available; (7) The modernization of equipment at the international communications center in Almaty and at the automated trunk telephony stations in Uralsk, Taraz, Aktobe, and Astana was completed. The international communications center in Astana was built and opened in September 2001. It has allowed completion of a digital trunk communications network; (8) The introduction of new digital telephone stations with total built-in capacity of 500,000 numbers in cities and 200,000 numbers in rural areas; (9) The expansion of the network of universal pay phones up to 6,600 units while replacing all token-based pay phones with card-based phones; and (10) The construction of a third international communications center in Aktobe.

PSTN (Public Switch Telephony Network)

PSTN has a high strategic importance in the telecommunications industry. PSTN includes 3,009 local ATs, 21 trunk stations, and two international stations. PSTN is based on a first-level network embodying the whole territory of Kazakhstan and providing access to international ports. The first-level network consists of switching stations, transmission equipment, access equipment, and telephony lines. At the beginning of 2001, the first-level network included 102.5 thousand km of air-borne lines, and 137.2 thousand km of cable lines (including 24.2 thousand km of fiber-optic cable). PSTN has a three-level hierarchical structure, local, regional (intra-zone), and trunk networks. The total length of trunk telecommunication networks equaled 37.9 thousand km in late 2000, including 25.2 thousand km of cable and 12.6 thousand km of radio-relay lines. Kazakh Telecom has the exclusive rights to use PSTN, trunk, and international networks in exchange for obligations to develop service in rural areas, which are unprofitable. Being the sole owner of PSTN, Kazakh Telecom is actually a monopolist in the area of voice telephony service. Structurally, the system in many market segments has to be connected through a national operator. For instance, cellular communication service operators achieve connection with Kazakhstan's telephone network only by means of PSTN.

Cable Owners

Such large operators as Ducat (the united trademark of Arna, Rate, and Kazintel) and Astel have their own fiber-optic lines. These lines give them the ability to operate mostly in business-to-business environments. There is a growing trend among business customers in the telecommunications market toward demanding a wider range of services. Ducat's telecommunication networks include fiber-optic and satellite connection lines. Ducat digital network applies advanced telephony stations that allow for high quality local, trunk, and international communication; rapid configuration of corporate nets with any amount of telephone numbers; prioritized access to trunk and international communications; and high-speed access to the Internet.

Ducat networks interact with the global communication and information networks. Ducat offers its customers a direct access to international communication channels with the biggest communication operators—British Telecom, Telstra, and Sovintel. International ports are located in Almaty, Atyrau, and Aksay.

Astel Company (formerly Arna Sprint Data Communications) has operated in the Kazakhstani market since 1993 and has its representative offices in all areas of Kazakhstan. Astel has created Kazakhstan's first integrated telecommunications network (KazNet) for general-use data transmission based on high-speed fiber-optic cables and satellite communications. KazNet is integrated in a worldwide net, Global One, which has up to 1000 points of presence throughout the world. Astel has a developed infrastructure made up of integrated telecommunication networks and regional branches. The company's telecommunications network has been built on a base of speedy trunks using advanced equipment. KazNet is connected through fiber-optic and satellite channels with the EQUANT network, a global Internet network. KazNet has locks into domestic and international networks.

Data Transmission Service and Internet Service Providers (ISP)

Due to growing demand, Internet service providers, voice over internet protocol (VOIP) providers, and developers of software applications all show stable growth. The main first-level providers (providers who have direct access to global Internet providers) are Kazakh Telecom, Nursat, Arna, and Astel. The number of second-level providers (providers who offer access to the Internet through the first-level providers) was more than 100 in 2002. (Generally, the lower the level the provider is, the lower the quality of connections will be.)

Significant growth in sales of VOIP telephony service is expected. This will be the result of companies striving to go around Kazakh Telecom, the monopolist in traditional telephone service. VOIP telephony is an attractive alternative since it allows for reduced costs. However, the quality of VOIP telephony is quite low, typically with time delays and frequent loss of signal.

Satellite Communications

The satellite communications market in Kazakhstan is growing with the demand for improved telecommunications services and infrastructure. Telecommunications providers offer various services to its customers in Almaty, regional centers, and in the remote areas not provided with international telephone access by other means—satellite earth stations; VSAT's (very small aperture terminals); international private lines; mobile satellite phones (Inmarsat); payphones; etc. Customers mostly include multi-national corporations, oil and gas companies conducting exploration work in remote areas, Kazakhstani and foreign governmental entities, and businesses.

Currently, Kazakh Telecom uses four Intelsat satellites and has four earth stations in different parts of the country. Kazakhstan's Intelsat signatory is the Ministry of Transportation, Communications, and Tourism (MTCT) with Kazinformtelecom as the investing entity. The MTCT granted rights for using the Intelsat system to Kazakh Telecom and three private firms—Kazinformtelecom, Rahat Telecom (Kazakhstani), and Nursat (a U.S.-Kazakhstani joint venture).

Two receiving stations for satellite telecommunications systems have been built in Almaty—Intelsat Standard F3 and Intelsat Standard A. An Orbita earth station has been built in Astana. Standard F1 and Standard F2 satellite earth stations in Atyrau Oblast and a Standard G earth station in Aktau have been built to provide communication services to major oil and gas companies in the region. In addition to Intelsat, Kazakh Telecom works with the global satellite system's regional competitors—Intersputnik (a former Soviet bloc satellite system), Turksat (a Turkish satellite company), and Eutelsat (the European satellite system).

There are a number of communications companies which operate in other-than-Intelsat systems. Among them are Jarykh and TNS-Plus. Jarykh is Kazakhstan's satellite communications operator and the accounting authority and routing organization for Inmarsat in Kazakhstan. It has five joint ventures with American, British, and Indonesian telecom companies. TNS-Plus provides services through Inmarsat and VSAT satellites.

Microwave Communications

In the area of microwave communications, a large network provides radio communication services, with stations transmitting in short-, medium- and long-wave bands, as well as in FM. The modernization of the existing microwave lines began with the installation of new equipment working on the digital transmission principle. Among the suppliers of microwave equipment are Motorola, Icom, YaesuNetex, Kenwood, Seslecton, Codan, and SGC.

Trunked Communications

Trunked communication service is widely used in Kazakhstan. Customers of this service include governmental entities and businesses, representative offices of foreign companies, police, taxis, courier services, as well as Western oil companies conducting exploration in remote areas. Suppliers of terminal equipment include Motorola, Icom, Ericsson,

Simoco, and Maxon. Among suppliers of the equipment for base stations are Motorola, Nokia, and Tait. Future development plans for some of the service providers call for combining trunked networks in the cities and in the oil fields into a single network, and providing roaming throughout the Republic.

Wireless Local Loop

Digital radio access in CDMA standard is used by Instaphone, a U.S. and Kazakhstan joint venture with Metromedia, to provide subscribers with the following services: wireless local telephone service; wireless point-to-multipoint data transmission; wireless fixed access to voice service; wireless fixed access to data networks; and wireless fixed access to ISDN networks. Alcatel, Airspan Communication, and InnoWave ECI Telecom provide equipment for this kind of telecommunications.

Paging

In May 1999, there were 22 paging operators in Kazakhstan, providing their services in almost all of the regional centers. Service providers use the equipment of Motorola, Philips, LG, Samsung, and others. Paging services are widely used by businesses and private individuals alike. There are certain difficulties in this sector. The main one is that a large number of subscribers constantly change operators, seeking more beneficial service conditions. Also, the monthly payment for pagers and the cheapest cellular phones are approximately the same. This is forcing paging service providers to find new ways to attract clients.

Human Resource Management

The strategy is to achieve a highly skilled workforce in the industry; the objectives are to provide government financial support (grants and credit) for students attending local institutes (15% of the total budget); to provide a high educational level in local institutes (every year providing training for institute teachers abroad); and (for each telecom company) to provide training courses for employees in CIS countries and abroad. The policies are: to increase the educational level of experts and specialists by means of international cooperation in information exchange, and by holding workshops and implementing joint programs; and to see that there are special courses (learning centers at manufacturers of telecommunications equipment, grants and credits for high schools in CIS countries, and training within telecommunication companies) to provide certain kinds of needed specialists in a timely manner.

In Closing

The Ministry of Transport and Communications significantly regulates Kazakhstan's telecommunications industry. An important reform-oriented, step-by-step liberalization of operators' rights is underway. As a result, continued restructuring of the telecommunications industry is expected. The dominant player in this industry is Kazakh Telecom, which has already accumulated considerable potential in technology and human resources, and has a developed network infrastructure. Besides its direct presence in the market, Kazakh Telecom is also represented through its shares in other companies. Other large telecommunications companies are: Nursat, Ducat, TNS Plus, Astel, Catelco, and Golden Telecom. Departmental operators are Kaztranscom, Transtelecom, and Kazaeronavigatsiya. Cellular communications service operators are Altel, GSM-Kazakhstan, and Kar-Tel. These companies have already been in the market for a long time and operate in various niches. Ducat is part of a foreign company, ERDB. As a subsidiary it has access to extra financial resources, international contracts, and technologies. Golden Telecom has its own access to international networks, which gives it a leading role as an operator of Internet traffic. Ownership of telecommunications networks is a key advantage in the industry.

Figure 9-1
Total Revenue from Traditional Telephony in 2002

Services	Market Volume In billion tenge
International calls	7.0
CIS	8.0
Kazakhstan	16.0
Local	11.5
Total	42.5

Source: National Statistics Agency of Kazakhstan

Figure 9-2
Strategic Analysis

Strengths	Weaknesses
☐ Intensifying investments in development ☐ Wide range of services ☐ Operational cost reduction ☐ Equipment from world suppliers ☐ Competitive quality in Almaty ☐ International training programs	☐ Poorly developed infrastructure ☐ Low population density ☐ Inadequate number of digital lines ☐ Monopolization ☐ Weak legislation base ☐ Lack of qualified personnel ☐ Low quality

Opportunities	Threats
☐ Strategic industry ☐ Geographical position ☐ Demonopolization ☐ Increase of income level ☐ Increase of user base	☐ Slowing economy ☐ Brain Drain ☐ Government deregulation ☐ Demonopolization ☐ Substitute products ☐ Inflation rate

Figure 9-3
Comparison of Charges for Telecommunication Services
(2003)

Type of Services	Unit of measurem't	Trans-telecom	Kazakh telecom	Ducat	Nursat	Astel
Local network						
Setting up phone	Tenge	43,000	43,000	43,000	78,000	-
Customer payment	Tenge	750	950	950	4,992	-
Inter-area network						
1 zone	Tenge/sec	11	16	16	109	NA
2 zone	Tenge/sec	12	18	16	109	NA
3 zone	Tenge/sec	13	20	16	109	NA
4 zone	Tenge/sec	15	24	16	109	NA
5 zone	Tenge/sec	16	25	16	109	NA
International network						
Russian	Tenge/sec	-	153	55	109	94
CIS countries	Tenge/sec	-	153	55	109	101
Europe	Tenge/sec	-	230	184	140	117
USA	Tenge/sec	-	230	184	140	117
Access to the Internet	Tenge/hr.	-	184	158	208	304
Special line access to the Internet						
Connection	Tenge	-	94,341	-	101,400	191,100
Consumer payment 64 Kbyte/sec	Tenge/mo.	-	52,156	-	28,080	65,520
For traffic	Tenge/100 MB	-	1,841	-	1,716	2,028
Access to the Internet through ADSL						
Connection	Tenge	-	46,020	62,700	-	-
Consumer payment 64 Kbyte/sec	Tenge/mo.	-	52,156	35,000	-	-
For traffic	Tenge/100 MB	-	1,841	1,900	-	-

Source: National Statistics Agency of Kazakhstan

Figure 9-4
Telecommunication Industry Revenues
(million Tenge)

	1999	2000	2001	2002
Revenue from Main Communication Activity, (at current prices)	32,278	42,494	68,279	90,317
Revenues from Communication Services Rendered to Population	12,573	16,013	25,635	33,324

Source: Statistical Bulletin, National Statistics Agency of Kazakhstan

Conclusion

As we have discussed, Kazakhstan is a very large country blessed with rich natural resources. After her independence, one would expect her to be doing much better, but her progress has been rather slow. From an economic point of view, Kazakhstan still lags very much behind other newly independent nations, particularly in the area of manufacturing, which is critical for a healthy economy for any society, and there is no valid reason for not developing the sector. The consumers' over-dependence on imported goods is very disturbing; particularly since they do not seem to care. Why aren't they doing something about starting their own garment industry, or making toys, and furniture, etc.? And how about processing agricultural products by themselves? What will happen when the rich natural resources diminish sometime in the future?

Why not use her rich resources to hire experts from advanced countries now to have them evaluate and analyze the situation, and determine what can be done, and should be done, to get started on building a foundation for future prosperity? How long can Kazakhstan continue what she is doing now, having three-quarters of her working population working for the government? It is imperative that Kazakhstan build a balanced economic foundation. In the past eighteen years, many other independent nations have made significant progress, but how about Kazakhstan? Does the government have a concrete and sound five- or ten-year plan to build a balanced economic structure? Are the leaders doing their best to use the most competent people for the betterment of the society? They need to shed the antiquated Soviet mind-set and accept meritocracy so that the best and brightest can develop their abilities to the fullest and serve the country. That should be the most urgent major concern for the government and leaders.

As we know, each society goes through an adaptation process when any new knowledge is introduced, whether developed within, or diffused from another society. When the adaptation of the new knowledge is successful, it benefits the society, and many changes will follow. An adaptation process is selective, and if a new knowledge is a technological one, usually it is accepted and adopted by the receiving society, because usually its impact would be beneficial, such as making life a little easier, etc., and, at least not threatening to the cultural core, such as the value systems, of the society.

On the other hand, if a new knowledge is an ideology or related to the society's value system, the receiving society is usually cautious, e.g., anti-Marxism in the West and other societies in the twentieth century, often with a government intervention, because such ideology threatens the basic institutions of the society. Even when it's their own invention, how it is used is selective and depends on the society's culture, particularly the value system. For example, fireworks in China: even though the Chinese knew it could be used as a gun powder, they refused to use it for that purpose, and kept the knowledge just for the beauty of fireworks. But, the West gained the knowledge and immediately used it to make guns.

In the case of Kazakhstan, the Soviet system was imposed and thus diffused into Kazakhstan's culture, and changed the entire way of life of the society. A given society's culture, at any given time, is an end result of all past adaptation processes, thus resulting in the differences of cultures in the world. For Kazakhstan, her natural cultural change and development were interrupted by the Soviets. In addition, with the vast area and its unique geographic environment, Kazakhstan remained as mostly nomadic tribal societies, and did not become a sedentary society with private ownership of the land and a central government. That is, she did not go through the usual progression, from a hunting-gathering society to the horticultural level and a sedentary society, where division of labor began to develop, followed by the early agricultural level, and industrialization, leading to the post-industrial society of today. That means the usual development of most societies, including manufacturing activities, did not take place in Kazakhstan before the Soviet Union took over. As a part of the Soviet system, Soviet leaders wanted to take advantage of Kazakhstan for her natural resources, as any typical colonial power, and sold what was produced. So the development of Kazakhstan was not as an independent nation. Therefore, it was left in that stage.

Unless the people in Kazakhstan themselves are fully aware of that historical fact, as well as what is going on outside the Soviet-controlled areas now, they may not think of catching up by themselves. That is a serious problem for the country. If the current leaders are still very much of the Soviet mentality, then what could we expect? In other words, when Kazakhstan was finally freed from that deprivation from the natural progression of her economy, the people should learn and do what is required for the society to build an independent and/or sustainable economy.

What was needed when Kazakhstan gained her independence was for her new leaders to send their brightest young people to the world's leading countries to evaluate where they themselves were, and to learn what they should do for their future. All the problems the new government must deal with are not new to the world: other societies have dealt with them, some successfully, some not. Why not learn from other's successes and failures? There is no need to try and err all over. While the nation is still lucky enough to be able to count on her rich natural resources, which would give them a little extra time, they should use that wealth to do whatever is necessary for the future of the nation—to analyze what they should develop first, etc. Some of the problems may be more basic, such as how to make the best use of their huge land, and how the water may need desalination technology, etc., etc. Some such problems may commonly be shared by other societies. The government needs to make the best use of the available knowledge in the world, both natural scientific and social scientific, so that the society can make the best use of her material wealth and human resources.

Regrettably, one serious problem that Kazakhstan is facing is an illicit drug problem, of being a major heroin smuggling route, transporting cocaine produced in Afghanistan and nearby regions to Russia and Europe, and also producing marijuana in Kazakhstan's mountain areas, which is said to be worth as much as a billion US dollars. Currently, the government, with a well-trained special task force, is trying very hard to combat the problem, but it seems to be a losing battle as long as the ordinary citizens do not reject such business firmly and/or allow the illicit activities involved with the Russians to continue in their country. Perhaps the development of Kazakhstan's basic industry might attract her people more to engage themselves with national pride, with constructive activities such as manufacturing, excavation of natural resources and the refinery business, transportation activities, as well as education, judicial, artistic, and a variety of all other productive activities including working for the government. Their national pride, as well as their self-respect, perhaps, will put a brake on such illicit activities and possibly help it to end. Kazakhstan certainly does not need drug-related activities.

For that reason as well, it is critical that the manufacturing industry be developed as fast as possible. There is no reason, no obstacles, for the lack of such basic activities, e.g., the garment industry, and other basic manufacturing activities. Just because they have oil and gas monies, why should they keep importing clothing, first from China, which is now being replaced by Turkey (after Chinese-made outfits caused health problems), and other countries? Using the monies from natural resources, why not invite some foreign managers as advisers to start a variety of manufacturing businesses? It will not be very difficult to start manufacturing bases for garments, food processing, toys, office supplies, furniture, electronics, etc., and that development will even lead to construction and retailing businesses, and also will support oil, gas, copper, and other natural resource businesses with their refining sector.

So far, the majority of foreign direct investments in Kazakhstan have been to the oil and gas industries. Currently the members of OPEC and Russia have political clout in the global energy markets, but Kazakhstan is not a major player in geopolitics. And that is the problem. Not only does Russia have huge oil and gas reserves of her own, but she is also still controlling the refining capacities of Kazakhstan's gas and oil, as well as some of the flows of refined oil to the world market. So, what Kazakhstan needs to do is to upgrade the infrastructure for both the gas and oil industries, but for that she needs to improve supply chain management and other areas of business by improving personnel training. In other words, it is important for Kazakhstan to train young people to be well educated, not only technologically but also in the field of human relations, as well as a broad liberal arts background so that they can think analytically, and make the best decisions possible, based on the best knowledge available, using mature and wise judgment. For that, strengthening the educational system which includes more broadly educated young people, not limited in management, is extremely important for Kazakhstan in order to be able to compete with other countries in the generations to come. Kazakhstan should stop behaving as if she were still part of the Soviet system.

So, what is needed in Kazakhstan is a very broadly educated, analytical-thinking leader, with a great respect for Kazakhstan and her past, who can shed the remaining antiquated Soviet mind-set and value system. Unless that happens, Kazakhstan will remain a nation with a very high tolerance for corruption and the business mentality for quick money, i.e., lack of integrity, and over-dependence on the government, i.e., lack of initiative, which leads to a lack of self-respect. All of that is extremely hazardous for the nation's future. Marxism was quite adaptive long ago for early agricultural society and/or early industrial society because of the nature of the work for the most part, but not for the post-industrial society of today, which requires so much knowledge and intelligence for the majority of work instead of manual labor. Moreover, as a land-locked country, it is understandable that the leaders of today are still catering to Russia, as an old habit dies slowly, but it is of utmost importance that the leaders should develop, or be replaced by new leaders, with the ability to negotiate with neighboring nations on an equal standing, intelligently, with a thorough knowledge of not only events around them but also the world in general, with integrity and dignity. The entire society's institutions must adapt themselves to meet that challenge.

At any rate, unfortunately, the people in Kazakhstan were kept isolated from the free world for so long that they have no idea of the reality of the world, and how things are done outside the Soviet Union. So they are not even aware of the extent to which they have been deprived by the Soviets, let alone the damage caused by the Soviets, which they have tolerated, but are not accepted by the rest of the world's standard.

Now that the people are independent and associating with the rest of the world, and newly established universities are doing their best, I am hopeful that they will catch up with the rest of the world, make the best use of the country's natural resources, including her vast land, and develop a fine, affluent society.

A famous National Poet and Scholar, Abai Kunanbaev, during the the 19th century, expressed the culture of the inhabitants of latter half of Kazakhstan—through poetry—and was able to synthesize the wisdom of the East and the progressive ideas of the West. In the same vein, he also developed the Western-Eastern synthesis of Goethe, while opposing vehemently the colonization concepts of "Eurocentric" and nationalistic pursuits. In Abai's poetry, we see the highest spiritual values and the concept of freedom against social evil and inhumanity. We find similar characteristics in the writings of Shakespeare, Goethe, Byron, and Pushkin. Abai was often too critical of his fellow men. Even to this day, Abai's creative poetry influences the thinking of educated Kazakhs. The following poem describes his feelings and closeness to his people:

I spoke many words before too,

In sadness I spoke them, thinking of the future,
Hoping that the intelligent ones would be ashamed
And think again and try to turn over a new leaf.
Our people talk too much; they're not a good example.
One word hastens after another—there's no
                              Understanding them.
With tears from eyes, with blood from heart—
It's impossible to thaw the ice of their souls.
O, my people, don't be so arrogant, listen.
Don't think about the external form of words,
Concentrate on their sense—what does it cost you to
                              Listen a little?

These words are not written for idle talk.
Don't get lost off the road.
Get onto and stick to the beaten track.
No knowledge, no work.
You've forgotten how to pasture the herds.

References

Chapter 1
How Kazakhstan's Present Competes with Past Values

1. National Statistical Agency of Kazakhstan, 2002.
2. The Library of Congress Country Studies, 2003.

Chapter 2
Kazakhstan's Oil Supply Chain Management Challenges

1. Birol, F. (2006). World energy prospects and challenges. *The Australian Economic Review*, vol. 39, no. 2, pp. 190-195.
2. Bud La Londe. (2006). Energy problem cries for decisive action. *Supply Chain Management Review*, Vol. 10, Issue 6, p. 6.
3. Cavenagh, A. (1999, February 24). Caspian Oil Project Has a Slow Road to Syndication. *Project Finance International*, 50-51.
4. Cavinato, J. (2002, May-June). What's your supply chain type? *Supply Chain Management Review,* 60-66.
5. Chopra, S. and Meindl, P. (2004). *Supply Chain Management* (Second Edition). New Jersey: Prentice-Hall.
6. *Doing Business with Kazakhstan.* (2004). Edited by Marat Terterov. London, England: Kogan Page Publishers.
7. Feiveson, H. (1998). *The problem of Caspian energy.* Princeton, New Jersey: Princeton University.
8. Gaudenzi, B. and A. Borghesi. (2006). Managing risks in the supply chain using AHP method. *International Journal of Logistics Management*, vol. 17, 114-136. www.gravmag.com
9. Lee, Hau L. (2002). Aligning supply chain strategies with product differentiation. *California Management Review*, 105-119.
10. Lockamy, A. and Kevin McCormack. (2004). Linking SCOR planning practices to supply chain performance. *International Journal of Operations & Production Management*, vol. 24, 1192-1218.
11. National Statistics Agency of Kazakhstan, 2005. www.petroleumjournal.kz
12. Rasizade, A. (1999). Azerbaijan, the U.S., and oil prospects on the

Caspian Sea. *Journal of Third World Studies*, vol. XVI, No. 1, 29-48.
13. Report of Baker and McKenzie. (2002, November). *CIS Energy Notes*.
14. Report of KazakhOil (2005).
15. Sridharan, U., Caines, R. and C. Patterson. (2005). Implementation of supply chain management and its impact on the value of firms. *Supply Chain Management*, Vol. 10, 313-318.
16. Yergin, D. (2007). Oil market fever as prices near $100. *Pipeline & Gas Journal*, Issue II, p. 97-98.

Chapter 3
The Gas Industry: Infra-structural Challenges

1. "Leadership is Not Eternal," Shell, *Medvezhiy Ugol* magazine, 6-7 (23-24), 2001.
2. "Caspian" journal, Gas industry of Kazakhstan, October 2000.
3. Russian Natural Gas resources and northeast Asia: Deposits-Development-Delivery Trilemma" (Reflections on the conference debates and informal talks in Yakutsk, Vladimir I. Ivanov, Research Division, Erina.
4. Michael Wilson & Partners, Presentation on the gas industry of Kazakhstan.
5. Andrey Chursov, BISNIS Representative, Almaty, Kazakhstan, August 8, 2001.
6. "Oil and Gas: the return of geopolitics," Annual Meeting, World Economic Forum, January 26, 2001.
7. "Kazmunaigaz" presentation at KIOGE 2002, Almaty.
8. "Gas Industry of Kazakhstan," Joklybai Egizbayev, *Caspian Journal*, October 2000.
9. World Bank, "Report on Gas and Power Privatization in Hungary and Kazakhstan."
10. Karachaganak Integrated Organization.
11. "Kazakhstan's GDP grows by 9.5 percent in 2002," Reuter, February 7, 2003.
12. "Gas Industry of Kazakhstan," *Caspian*, 2003.
13. "Minister of Energy and Natural Resources Shkolnik predicts overproduction of natural gas," Interfax, January 2003.
14. "Industry of the Republic of Kazakhstan, Statistics for 1990-1997," 1998, p. 115. "Industry of the Republic of Kazakhstan and Regions, Statistics for 1990-1998," p. 53. "Social and Economic Situation in the Republic of Kazakhstan," Jan-Dec 1999, 2000, pp. 130-157.
15. Source: Kazakhstan: Development of the new gas field, International Copyright, US & Foreign Commercial Service and US Department of State, 2001.

16. Interfax Newsletter, January 3, 1998, p. 11.
17. "BP signs a gas deal in Kazakhstan," Reuters, 1997.
18. Interfax News, March 8, 2003.
19. *Financial Times*, 2003.
20. Itar-Tass, January 2003.
21. World Economic Forum Annual Meeting, 2001.
22. Kazakhstan: Development of the new gas field, International Copyright, US & Foreign Commercial Service and US Department of State, 2001.

Chapter 4
The Transportation Industry:
Where Modernity and Mobility Benefit Kazakhstan

1. Transport in the republic of Kazakhstan. Statistical data. Almaty, 2001.
2. http://web.worldbank.org/
3. Ibid.
4. Panorama, #11, March 21, 2003.
5. Transport of the Republic of Kazakhstan. Statistical data, 2001.
6. ww.kazakhstan-gateway.kz/economy/transport
7. www.portaktau.kz
8. Strategy of Development of Kazakhstan 2003.
9. www.stat.kz
10. www.stat.kz
11. Panorama 12.11.02.
12. Panorama, #11, March 21, 2003.
13. "Transportation infrastructure of Republic of Kazakhstan" – report for IV International conference TRANSEUROASIA – 2002.
14. http://www.kabar.kg/english/fei/2001/5/31.html May 31, 2001 "Kyrgyzstan and ADB signed agreement on reconstruction of Bishkek-Almaty highway."
15. http://web.mit.edu/esd.83/www/notebook/transportation
16. Panorama 14.03.03.
17. http://www.astanet.com/
18. Roland H. Ballou, *Business Logistics Management: Planning, Organizing, and Controlling the Supply Chain*, Prentice-Hall, 4th Edition, 2000, p. 157.
19. http://web.worldbank.org/
20. "Trans-Euroziya-2002" International Trade in Kazakhstan, IV International Conference, Astana, 2002.
21. Ibid.
22. Ibid.

Chapter 5
The Retail Industry:
Recent Development in Kazakhstan

1. http://www.statebase.kz/
2. Alan Dion, "New strategies for the future European utilities market," ECTU 2000, pp. 15-23.

Chapter 6
The Copper Industry:
A Quasi-Privatization at Work in
Post-Soviet Republic of Kazakhstan

Interviews of managers of Kazakhmys Corporation,
    Representatives in Almaty
IRBIS Agency
National Statistics Agency
Agency of the Republic of Kazakhstan on Investments
www.Kazakhmys.kz
Denton Wilde Sapte, Legal overview mining Kazakhstan
www.alwaysmining.com
www.miningandevents.com
www.Copperinfo.com
www.oko-kz.com/Arhiv
www.mineral.ru
www.Kazakhstan_gateway.kz
Almanac.ods.org/Kazakhstan
www.Minikz.com/mining
user.bigpord.com/ausmines/copperspotprices
www.metal.merge.com/mm/news
www.emergingmarkets.com/kazkommerts
www.president.kz/articls/economy
www.mineral.ru
www.kommersant.ru
www.infogeo.ru
Eurasia.metals/2002/copper
www.kase.kz
Euramet.ru/online
www.okno.com/actfig/kazakhstan.html
www.geocities.com/yerdik/kzinfo.html
www.kazakinfo.com/economy
www.mined_copper.html
Mullins, Marcy E., "Copper plunges," *USA Today*, June 17, 1997, p. 4B.

Chapter 7
The Construction Industry:
Internationalization and Growth

1. Delovaya Nedelya, #32, 2002.
2. Kazakhstanskaya Pravda, #24, 2002.
3. Construction in Kazakhstan, Statistic Issue, p. 45.
4. National Statistics Agency
5. Ibid.
6. Kazakh State Architecture and Construction Academy archives
7. N.A Nazarbayev, "Kazakhstan 2003," p. 42.
8. National Statistics Agency
9. Construction in Kazakhstan, Statistic Issue, p. 30.
10. Construction in Kazakhstan, Statistic Issue, p. 43.

Chapter 9
Telecommunication: Where Global Trends Dominate

1. Nazarbaev N. Kazakhstan – 2003. President of the country' message to the people of Kazakhstan. Almaty. 1997, p. 151.
2. Nazarbaev N. Kazakhstan – 2003. President of the country' message to the people of Kazakhstan. Almaty. 1997, p. 151; b) Web site: www. mkt.gov.kz
3. Nazarbaev N. Kazakhstan – 2003. President of the country' message to the people of Kazakhstan. Almaty. 1997, p. 153.
4. Interview: Jef Andrusevich, WorldCom director, office in Almaty.
5. Web site: www. mkt.gov.kz
6. Ibid.
7. Tashimova N. Organizational factors of development of telecommunication service market. Transitnaya economica. Almaty. 2002, p. 99.
8. Kazakhstan On line: (Telecommunication). Securities market. Almaty. 2001, p. 32.
9. Kazakhstan: 1991-2002. Informational analytical collection. Agency on Statistics of the republic of Kazakhstan/ Edited by AA.Smailova/ Almaty. 2002, p. 340-353.
10. Interview with employees from Transtelecom Erick Essengaliev; www.kazakhtelecom.kz
11. Kazakhstan Online: (Telecommunication). Securities market. Almaty. 2001, p. 32.
12. Internet. Web site. www.mtk.gov.kz

13. Statistical Bulletin. Agency of statistics of the Republic of Kazakhstan. Edited by A. Smailov. Almaty. 2003, p. 38.
14. Statistical Bulletin. Agency on Statistics of the Republic of Kazakhstan. Edited by A. Smailov. Almaty. 2003, p. 37-39.

Index